A BAKER'S DOZEN!

A
BAKER'S
DOZEN!

Thirteen tasty morsels to chew over!

CHRIS HILL

CL Publications

𝒞 ℒ Publications

28 Thorney Road, Capel St Mary, Suffolk IP9 2LH

Copyright © Christopher Hill

First Published 2016

Unless otherwise stated, Scripture quotations are taken from the HOLY BIBLE, New International Version. Copyright © 1973, 1978, 1984 by International Bible Society.
KJV – King James Version. Crown Copyright.

Cover design and print production for the publisher by Gipping Press Ltd., Needham Market, Suffolk IP6 8NZ

ISBN: 978-0-9954736-1-4

CONTENTS

INTRODUCTION

This series of thirteen essays began life as articles written for *SWORD Magazine* and are presented in book form with the generous permission of the Editor, David Andrew.

In my Introduction to a previous book, *Built for Battle*, I referred to the Coat of Arms of one of our great Naval Commanders, Admiral Jackie Fisher. It reads, *"Fear God and dread nought"*. What a fitting motto also for disciples of Jesus Christ!

As we progress through these Last Days, there is much to concern us. Not only the seemingly irrepressible march of Islam and rank atheism, but also the wholesale falling away from the Bible that is undermining churches at an alarming rate. The two-prong attack of the enemy, from outside and inside, fills us with growing alarm and yet so many believers give every indication that they are impotent and have little inclination to stand against it. We could go further and say there is every indication of a tacit unwillingness to acknowledge either prong of Satan's strategy and so we watch, rooted to the spot, as disaster creeps ever closer.

You may say, "Chris, you're being melodramatic and somewhat paranoid!" I only wish that were the case. But I fear it is not. True Christians are in trouble and we need help and encouragement 'big time'.

SWORD Magazine provides that level of help and encouragement and I feel privileged to be associated with it. If you are not yet a subscriber, I urge you to become one. Contact the editorial team at
290 Moston Lane, Manchester M40 9WB. Tel: 0844 4140618
E mail: subscribers@swordmagazine.co.uk.

Needless to say I have been truly blessed by having the encouragement and unflagging support of Lindy, my super-spouse and a band of supporters and intercessors who keep me focused on my calling: *"Thou art a preacher of the Word: mind thy business!"*

I trust this little offering of thirteen essays may act to make you think, if necessary lead you to repent and then set you on your way to victory!

Fear God and dread nought!

Chris Hill

Chapter One

Dare to be a Daniel

I loved Miss Chant. As I went "into Primary" on Sunday afternoons she used to give me a little coloured attendance stamp that she stuck into my stamp book. The stamps were in large sheets and Miss Chant tore them out very carefully one at a time as we all processed past her table, our footsteps clicking rhythmically as we sang *"... dropping, dropping, dropping, dropping, hear the pennies fall ...!"* I can still hear the chink of the coins as they fell through the slot and into the glass collection pot! Mind you, I'm not sure we fully understood the concept that *"... they belong to Jesus: He shall have them all!"* Did He come after Sunday School was over and remove them from the glass pot?

Dear Miss Chant is long gone, but I came across one of my stamp books the other day! It's seventy years old now ... but the memories linger!

One of my favourite stamps is Daniel in the lions' den. There he stands with eyes and hands uplifted in prayer, while the lions prowl round the den with a puzzled look on their faces as if saying to one another, *"Well, you guys, he looks juicy enough and we're pretty peckish, so why are we unable to pounce: feeling as if our hairy legs and paws are made of lead? It ain't natural!"*

1

The picture 'spoke' to me then when a four-year-old and it certainly speaks to me now, ageing juvenile that I am! There is something about Daniel that stirs the blood. He speaks to us across the running centuries. But then, so do many Bible characters and it is to be expected. The person who wrote the Letter to the Hebrews said as much. His catalogue of the faithful saints of the Hebrew Scriptures includes those who *"shut the mouths of lions and quenched the fury of flames"*. Their example is held out in order for *us* to stand firm under frightful provocation (Hebrews 12:1).

The Book of Daniel contains stirring accounts of brave men who deserve Heaven's accolade and it also contains astonishing, apocalyptic visions and dreams. The first half of the book describes the exciting adventures of Daniel and three of his friends, while the second half presents prophetic images: some of them very strange indeed. This perceived strangeness prevents some believers from studying the second half of the book … to their loss. The devil convinces them that anything even vaguely 'apocalyptic' should be avoided at all costs. *"After all"*, they say, *"we don't want to appear cranks and extremists, do we!"* What applies to Daniel Chapters 7-12 certainly applies to most of the Book of Revelation!

But never mind non-believers, for many of *us believers* these are imprisoned parts of the Bible!

Why is the devil so keen to steer us away from apocalyptic parts of Scripture? Probably because the Greek word *apokalupsis* means '*revelation*' or '*disclosure*'. Such revelation includes the glories of the coming Kingdom of God and discloses the strategy of the enemy against the servants of Jesus. Satan wants to keep us ignorant concerning his strategy and also his own coming demise at the hands of Jesus. Satan wants to keep us unprepared for the great spiritual battles of the End Times. In this subtle strategy he encourages the whole world to bury its collective head in the sand and to carry on regardless.

The Lord Jesus, on the other hand, wants to release us from ignorance, to reveal the present and future in order to give us understanding of the times: our clear and present dangers: and to enable us to prepare for battles ahead.

Unlike most other books of the Hebrew Scriptures, the Book of Daniel is not set in Israel. It is set in Babylon, in distant Mesopotamia, the land between the Rivers Tigris and Euphrates, hundreds of miles east of Jerusalem. How come?

Daniel Chapter 1 opens with the terrifying words,
"In the third year of the reign of Jehoiakim king of Judah, Nebuchadnezzar king of Babylon came to Jerusalem and besieged it."

It reads simply enough. The facts are stated succinctly. But it is impossible for us to imagine the horrors enshrined in those few words and felt by the besieged Jews as they cowered, trapped behind their city walls in the year 597BC.

The siege was a massive surprise to the people of Jerusalem, but it shouldn't have been. Jeremiah the prophet was just one who had warned for long enough that the spiritual lassitude of the Jews would have serious consequences. Repeated prophetic warnings had gone unheeded by government and people alike and now 'the chickens' had well and truly 'come home to roost'.

Through several generations the steady drip-drip of apostasy had eroded the Jews' faithfulness to the Lord God. Consequent disaster had struck ten years before in 607 when Nebuchadnezzar king of Babylon invaded Judah. It was the first in a series of three attacks spanning twenty years, the third of which in 586BC would result in the wholesale destruction of Jerusalem and its Temple and the exile of thousands of Jews northwards and eastwards across the Fertile Crescent and down into Babylon, the enormous pagan city that straddled the River Euphrates.

The Book of Daniel was written to encourage the Jewish people facing up to the rigours of exile and the culture shock produced by Babylonian daily life. It was dreadful for them. Gone were the securities of Temple worship, gone the mores of their fathers, gone the ever present reminders of the grace of God poured out upon the mountains and valleys of Judah, gone the faithful ministry of godly men like Jeremiah. All gone. Memories now and only memories.

Facing such an uncertain and dispiriting future was utterly appalling. Small wonder that in Psalm 137:1-4 the exiles cry out, *"By the rivers of Babylon, there we sat down; yes, we wept when we remembered Zion (Jerusalem). We hung our harps upon the willows in its midst. For those who carried us away captive required a song of us; and those who oppressed us required of us mirth, saying, 'Sing us one of the songs of Zion'. How will we sing the Lord's song in a strange land?"*

Coming to terms with the shattering realisation that we are dumped into an alien culture is never easy. We know! We're in it ... and *right* in it. So it is comforting to know that others have been there before us. And even more comforting to know that in that awful place, our Sovereign Lord has not left us!

Although it must have seemed to the Jews that their exile would have no end and that all was hopeless, it lasted for only seventy years. Just long enough for most of the generation that went into exile to have died. Some, however, would remain alive and migrate with the new generation back to Jerusalem under the leadership of Zerubbabel, Ezra and Nehemiah.

I'm not sure which is worse: being taken captive to a foreign land or being held captive by foreign powers in my own. Each is ghastly but it might even be worse to be forced to watch alien powers on the rampage, destroying one's own country before one's eyes. I don't like to contemplate that experience, do you? Yet it is becoming our *daily* experience now.

The rate of change to our culture is very fast. When I compare the Britain of today with the one I lived in seventy-plus years ago I scarcely recognise it. So much has changed and little for the better. It is pointless to catalogue the changes: we are all aware of them and they appear to impact every part of our personal and national life. All seems to be slithering downwards at an alarming rate and nobody has the wit or wisdom to halt the slide. It is like being in a foreign land and when we try to raise our voice in protest, alien voices scream us to silence. Satan is the ruler of this world, according to Jesus, and his cruel despotism is surely becoming more unbridled by the day.

It does no good to sit in the dust, home-sick, defeated and licking our wounds. We need to shake ourselves down and draw strength and encouragement from our true source of life – Jesus. His Word and Spirit can lift us into the Heavenlies where He dwells, so that whilst we languish here in our alien environment we are drawing our living breath from Him. He is the sustainer of our life.

I draw inspiration from Daniel and his three friends Hananiah, Mishael and Azariah. We may know the friends better by their Babylonian names Shadrach, Meshach and Abednego. Here were four Jewish lads sent to Babylon by Nebuchadnezzar as part of the first deportation of Jews in 607BC. The King had it in mind to train them as students at the University of Babylon, while at the same time wanting them to impart Jewish wisdom to his own students: trainee wise men that would enter his service in due course. He thought it a good arrangement.

As things turned out it was indeed a good arrangement. It meant that the four friends rose in Babylonian culture to such dizzy heights that they were able to guarantee the survival of the Jews in exile! In that respect their story is not unlike that of Queen Esther who lived not long afterwards.

The first challenge the four friends faced is recounted in Daniel 1. It concerned something as mundane as diet! Nebuchadnezzar wanted his trainees to be physically fit as well as mentally fit. So he saw to it that the students had the best food available … and believe me, it was *very* good! 'Cordon Bleu' doesn't even come close! Daniel and his friends were being plied with *royal* food: the finest fare that money could buy.

There was just one problem: much of it was not *kosher.* The food laws of the Mosaic Covenant forbade the eating of many things the Babylonians considered staples. So for Daniel and his friends to eat their splendid food would be to dishonour the Lord God of Israel and compromise their personal faith. But they had only just arrived in pagan Babylon! Best not upset anyone at this stage! Wasn't it a step too far? They were running a terrible risk!

It was doubly challenging because viewed from the Babylonian point of view the lads were being treated incredibly well. After all, they were *captives* and were fortunate to be alive let alone treated as favoured members of society.

The temptation was to be reasonable! You know how it goes: *"Why do you have to adopt this holier-than-thou attitude? When in Babylon do as the Babylonians do! In any event, eating only vegetables is not good for you and the King will see you looking pasty and we shall all cop it! Do us all a favour and tuck into the pork chops!"*

As we read the end of the story (Daniel 1:19-20) we see that God's way turned out to be the best way. When Nebuchadnezzar examined the lads he observed that their academic record was ten times better that that of their fellows. I don't think this was due to the diet, I believe it was due to what the diet represented: complete obedience to the Lord. That's the key to their success.

The first lesson Daniel had for God's people was that when we are called upon to contend with opposition from our captor-culture, it needs to be 'business as usual' no matter how great the provocation. Whether we are aware of it or not, the Lord is always with us. Hallelujah!

Chapter Two

Entering the Ministry

Words come and go. When I was a lad we used the word "smashing" quite a bit. A smashing girl, a smashing time, a smashing car, a smashing meal, a smashing football match … . Everything was "smashing"! It was the same with "jolly good"! Use those words today and people will cast an amused, indulgent glance at you as if you had just crept out of the Ark!

Words go … and words also come. A word used frequently now is "multi-tasking". According to my Chambers English Dictionary it is a computing term pertaining to a system capable of running several processes simultaneously. All clever stuff.

Just lately the word has been nudged across into the realm of human behaviour and a "multi-tasker" is a *person* who can do a number of jobs at the same time. Members of the fair sex are supposedly better at multi-tasking than we mere males. At any rate, that's what I hear.

Mind you, the concept of multi-tasking is not new to the Church. For a very long time it has provided a useful way to assess the quality of a Minister's success! If our Minister is not up to scratch in *every* aspect of ministry, he's not much cop and we'll pray for better things next time around!

If asked to list the qualities we would wish to find in our next Minister/Vicar/Pastor we may well include the following as essentials:

-   We want a good preacher and Bible teacher
-   We want a passionate evangelist
-   We want a deeply caring pastor
-   We want a wonderful visitor of the sick and elderly
-   We want an efficient administrator
-   We want a man of deep devotion who spends hours in prayer
-   We want a man who's good with young people and children
-   We want a man who's good with men *and* women
-   We want a man who spends time with other local clergy
-   We want a man who is *au fait* with modern technology
-   We want a man who is superb at relating to non-believers

In other words, we want a multi-tasker!

The question is, do such men exist in the Church? And if they do, *should* they exist?

As far as I can tell from reading the Bible, the only multi-tasker – the only omni-gifted person – is the Lord Jesus Himself! Nobody else is presented to us as being the embodiment of all the spiritual gifts and ministries. Even Paul the apostle did not consider himself to be more than a member of the corporate Body of Christ. Indeed he went out of his way to make the point on various occasions.

1 Corinthians 12:4-31 is a classic example where Paul shows multi-tasking to be quite an alien concept. We are to see ourselves as parts of the Body: each one functioning in his own particular gifting and – rather like an orchestra under the baton of the conductor – responding to the leading of the Holy Spirit as He directs things.

One Sunday recently I was preaching on 1 Corinthians 12:27, *"Now you are the body of Christ and individually members of it".* I was telling the congregation that every member of the Church needed to be aware of his or her particular gift and ministry in order for the active presence of Christ to be let loose.

The people greeted my message warmly. But then came the inevitable yet honest response from first one and then another. "I don't know what my ministry **is**, so how can I exercise it?" A further question then came up: "How do I discover what my spiritual gifts are?"

My answer was direct and to the point: "Ask the Lord to show you." After all, He is the One that gives His gifts and calls us to ministry. Does not the Word say, "If any of you lacks wisdom, he should ask God, who gives generously to all without finding fault, and it will be given to him. But when he asks, he must believe and not doubt …"?

So the first step is, ASK Father and expect an answer. This sounds well and good but so often it does not work out so easily. We pray and ask the Lord to show us our gifts and to reveal our ministry, but how are we expecting Him to do it?

The Bible often links a call to ministry with visions or words from Heaven: extraordinary events that are unmistakable. Such things *can* constitute a call by the Lord and when they do those receiving them usually write a book about it! The problem is that for most of us these singular and dramatic moments do not occur and then when we read the book we are floundering about in a sea of doubt, completely unaware of how we are to function as members of the body. It's all well and good for the author of the book, but what about **ME**?

Satan loves this scenario. He pumps us with doubt, guilt, self pity and anger that we have been sold short of what is our due. It works for others, but it doesn't work for me!

This produces a strong desire to hide away to nurse our grievance. "God, you don't love me like you seem to love these others!"

It may be helpful if I share my personal experience.

I was twenty years old when I asked the Lord to use me. I had been a Christian for two years. I asked and the Lord said nothing! On the basis that I knew He *wanted* me to ask Him, I persevered. He still said nothing. Then when I was twenty two and struggling with the whole question of guidance Lindy, my then fiancée, and I were invited to the Somerset town of Wiveliscombe to hear a well known preacher from London. He was Dr Martyn Lloyd-Jones.

His preaching pole-axed me. I had never heard anything so wonderful. The power of the Bible flowed through Lloyd-Jones, quickened by the Holy Spirit, and as it washed over me and through me, the Lord said, "Chris, this is what you are to be. I want you to preach My Word: to expound it faithfully and to turn from it neither to the right nor the left."

I was stunned. How could I possibly – a relatively uneducated young Somerset man – ever aspire to the heights of this man's ministry? The answer is that I never *could*! But that did not preclude me from aspiring to the heights of *my own potential ministry*! My Father did not require me to be a clone of "The Doctor", He wanted me to be *me*, but to be an expository preacher to the best of *my* personal ability, devoting myself to anything and everything that would make me a man of God who was steeped in the Scriptures.

So I would say the first stage was Father showing me what was truly in my heart and exposing the longing which had been lying dormant. He called it forth into the light when I saw another man doing it supremely well.

So I began to feed in God's Word. The first real opportunity I had to preach was to the National Young Life

Campaign group in Yeovil. I spoke about guidance by expounding Proverbs 3:5-6. The response was encouraging. Apparently the Holy Spirit brought conviction to the young people by opening God's Word to them. Such wonderful encouragement set me off on a pathway that has extended through fifty four years.

Please notice several things.
-       The first stage was that Father put a longing in my heart by exposing me to my ministry but expressed through another man.
-       The second was the testimony of believers who observed my ministry in action and who were touched by God in the process.
-       The third confirming sign was the Word itself. A highly respected and deeply committed Bible teacher gave me a Scripture verse that he felt was fitting for me. It was 2 Timothy 4:2, *"Preach the Word; be prepared in season and out of season; correct, rebuke and encourage – with great patience and careful instruction."*

So for me these elements have been helpful pointers for coming to an understanding of what my ministry truly is. I offer them to you.

1)   Ask Father to show you what He is calling you to and then try to discern the longing in your heart: what do you yearn to be?
2)   Look intently at the ministry of others and be open to the Lord saying at a particular moment, "This is for you too!"

3)   As you begin to make exploratory moves into that area of ministry, look for confirmation from those receiving it from you.

4)   Be alert to confirming Scriptures as you are studying the Word of God yourself and also as others give you particular verses they sense are for you.

I discovered that before firming up my call to be a preacher of the Word, the Lord wanted me to be devoted to the Scriptures and to Him. I would say this is the necessary preparation for all disciples of Jesus. During an interval between asking Father for a ministry and receiving the clarification as to what it is, it is vital that we become more and more committed to Him. This is a very unpopular instruction but it is time necessarily spent pursuing true godliness. Young Christians (of whatever age) always want immediate response from God. They do not understand that we must submit to periods of preparation. Such periods may be lengthy because much may need to happen in us first.

Consider the experience of Moses. He entered his true ministry when eighty years of age! Consider the experience of the Twelve. The apostles were taught and disciplined for three years by Jesus before they were ready for their ministries to be released. Someone once said, "Usually we believers are in a tearing hurry. Usually the Lord is not!"

Finally let's return to the matter of multi-tasking. I honestly cannot see a place for it in a biblical Church. The New Testament insists upon Body-ministry in which every member exercises his/her personal gifts as the Lord enables and calls.

If a believer reaches beyond his true calling into other areas of ministry which though attractive are not for him, two things usually result. First he will be distracted away from his true calling and end up feeling he has failed. Second he will feel threatened by those who are rightfully exercising the ministry he is mistakenly *trying* to fulfil. Both ways he is frustrated. Both ways he feels a failure. Joy goes from him and he feels himself to be on a treadmill of duty.

The Lord has a ministry for *you* to fulfil. You must discover it and pursue it with all your strength. The world is waiting for the true manifestation of Christ's life in His Church. You are a vital part of His strategy. Hallelujah!

Chapter Three

Ignore the Diversion signs!

I once overheard a conversation in which the subject of reading the Bible was being discussed.

"To be honest, there are many parts of the Bible I simply do not understand. I have real difficulty with those." So said one party, to which the other replied, "That's interesting. To be honest, I have real difficulty with the parts I *do* understand!"

It's easy to sympathise with both points of view, isn't it? Living with the Bible as the only rule of life is as demanding as it is unpopular. It can land us in very hot water at times. But there is nothing new in this for the determined disciple of Jesus.

'*Sola Scriptura*' was a vital note in the clarion call of the Reformation and it has echoed through the running centuries. As with all battle cries it is greeted with a mixed response. We either choose to pay attention and enter the lists or else we turn a deaf ear and carry on regardless!

This choice is as ancient as mankind. It was the choice faced by Adam in the Garden. Would he obey the voice of God or would he not?

It was the choice faced by our blessed Lord when confronted by Satan in the Wilderness of Judea. Luke 4:13 says, *"When the devil had finished all this tempting, he left Him until an opportune time."*

When was the opportune time? How long was our Lord spared the devil's attentions before the next round came? The answer can only be a matter of seconds! I say this because of Hebrews 4:15, where we are told He was *"tempted in every way, just as we are – yet without sin."*

So if our Lord's experience of temptation was like ours, it can only mean that He was the focus of the devil's attention *all the time!* Just like you and me! No sooner have I faced and come through one temptation when another sometimes of a quite different type rears its head and goes for me. As soon as I deal with that one, it seems yet another comes along hot on its heels!

So if this is to be my normal daily, moment by moment experience, how can I cope with it without falling headlong into temptation with monotonous regularity? The answer can only be, I do it like Jesus did it. For Him the choice was obvious: obey the Word of God or choose not to.

Every time Satan tempted our Lord, He responded in precisely the same way: *"It is written ... "*. Each time Jesus confessed the Scriptures. It is the *only* thing He did. *'Sola Scriptura'.*

Since my new birth I have always been an Evangelical. My simple definition of that is "someone who believes the Bible is entirely the Word of God and who seeks to live by every word of it." So when I was baptised in the Holy Spirit and began to exercise gifts of the Spirit it made not the slightest difference to my solid determination to be a Bible man. The two positions were entirely one.

After all, is this not one of the divine principles laid down in the foundation stones of God's self revelation? In Genesis 1:2 we are told that *"the Spirit of God was hovering over the waters."* Then again in verses 3, 5, 9, 11, 14, 20, 24 and 26 we find the recurring phrase, *"And God said ... ."* It introduces each Day of Creation. So if the creation power of God was released when His Spirit and His Word fused together, how could I possibly think they might be separated?

'Sola Scriptura' is a rallying battle cry to the storm-troopers of God, so we simply must listen and respond, living in the full truth and not fiddling about, playing fast and loose with inconvenient truth, which *though inconvenient is still truth!*

The fusion of Word and Spirit means the release of God's power. But it must be both. I have developed this in my CD set, "The Word, the Spirit and the Witnesses".

An astonishing example of true discipleship is shown in the life of Daniel (Daniel 1:1-17). He had been uprooted from his native land and replanted in pagan Babylon. There he was faced with the choice. The same choice that faced Peter and John centuries later when standing before the Sanhedrin. Their statement roars out like a klaxon: *"We must obey God rather than men!"* (Acts 5:29).

In 607BC, when Daniel was a teenager, Nebuchadnezzar brought the Babylonian army and lay siege to Jerusalem. He removed leaders and intelligentsia to Babylon. Daniel was among those exiles.

The contrast between famine-struck Jerusalem and the opulent splendour of Babylon could not have been greater. The new life style presented to Daniel was thoroughly pagan and the religious and moral restraints of home could have been forgotten very rapidly. Here was an opportunity for a new and fabulous lifestyle to be seized with both hands. Nebuchadnezzar was determined to re-educate Daniel in the ways of Babylon and clearly had high hopes of succeeding. After all, the new life presented to Daniel was the stuff of which dreams are made.

But Daniel's heart was set to please God. The pleasures of Babylon could easily have drawn him, but Daniel put purpose above passion and pleasure. Truth was vital so how could he stay true to the Lord? Daniel 1:8 says *"Daniel resolved not to defile himself with the royal food and wine."* His resolve could easily have resulted in death, but the Lord honoured it and honoured Daniel. That resolution not to defile himself is a powerful testimony. Would it not have been wiser and certainly reasonable to at least *sniff* or *sample* the King's food? Where could be the harm in that?

But the Word of God in regard to permitted food was very clear. As far as rich Babylonian fare was concerned it was off limits. *Completely* off limits.

The root of sin is *knowledge* of sin. We think we can indulge in the exploration of sin without being tainted by it. Just a look won't hurt: after all, it's *good* to know what we are to avoid!

This subtle approach is precisely that adopted by Satan in the Garden of Eden. The forbidden tree was not the tree of good and evil, but of the *knowledge* of good and evil (Genesis 2:16-17). Curiosity killed the cat! Even knowing and thinking about sin constitutes sin. That is why Daniel chose not to *know* about the sinful ways of Babylon.

Positive avoidance of stimulus to sin is a vital part of our armoury.

Wilf was a lovely guy. He had a terrible gambling problem when he came to us. My colleagues and I spent hours with him, praying for him and feeding Scripture into his life. All was going very well. Wilf was gaining the victory.

Then one day a little voice started whispering into his ear, "Wilf, you need to test this out." So Wilf got the local bus into town and made for the nearest Betting Shop. He stood across the road and looked at it, thankful that he had been released from his addiction. Then he crossed the road to *really* test it out. He watched men going in and out and heard the sounds with which he was so familiar. It was good to be free of it all. Then the little voice said, "You won't really know you're free unless you step inside the door, Wilf." Wilf listened and stepped inside ... He returned home to us later that afternoon a broken man. He had succumbed to the beguiling draw of the horses.

Have you ever wondered what people see in Internet pornography? Have you ever wondered what it's like? Wouldn't it be wise to *know* why so many Christian men are in thrall to it? After all, how can you understand and help people if you do not know why they are slaves to these things? It's not that you would become involved: it's simply a matter of *looking* ...

DO NOT DO IT!

A while ago Lindy and I were in Amsterdam. A well intentioned friend (not a believer) suggested I go with him to the Red Light district of the city to see why men are so tempted to go there and indulge their fantasies. He considered it would be a useful education for me. I began to consider it. I could easily see that such a visit would certainly give me many things and people to pray for. So perhaps it was a good idea. I DID NOT GO!

I know myself too well to dare to expose myself to such beguiling images. Lust would have had a field day with me, filling my mind with images that would taint my thought life for weeks to come.

There are occasions when I am taken by surprise with images and sounds that give rise to temptation and I have no control over their coming at me, but to deliberately put myself in harm's way is crazy and asking for trouble.

Daniel did not want to even know about the beguiling ways of Babylon. He understood – young though he was – that mere knowledge would have defiled him.

This kind of discipline is only possible for a man who is filled with the Word and filled with the Spirit, and there lies the challenge.

Daniel is impressive because he did not merely believe the truth of God's Word, he lived it. Uncomfortable truth or not, he lived it.

It has saddened me to see a shift taking place in churches and individuals who, though still calling themselves "Evangelical" have begun to depart from the faith. Time was when I considered the word "apostate" as applying to denominations that were governed by human reason and religious tradition rather than Scripture. But something has been creeping into Evangelicalism that I find very scary. There are beliefs and practices now widespread that fly in the face of the Bible. Many are so anxious to be on the wavelength of the society around us that they are compromising on even the most fundamental truths, even to the extent of permitting the precious doctrines of our redemption to be undermined.

Has the time come for us to make a stand for truth? But truth *applied*, not merely believed. Admittedly the word "Evangelical" does not appear in the Bible! What we call ourselves does not really matter that much, but biblical truth is unchanging and it is that which we must cling to, whatever label we choose to adopt. You can call yourself what you like, but the essential requirement is to be a man or woman who is 100% solid on the Scriptures and who is devoted to 100% submission to it, whatever the cost. Call me an extremist if you will: you are entitled to do that: but in the Lord's Name, PLEASE consider your position.

Chapter Four

All change!

"This is the 6 o'clock News … ."

Time was when I looked forward to the News on TV. But of late I rather dread it. If it's not bad news from the Middle East, Central Europe or Africa, it's bad news about terrorism, paedophilia, the killing of unborn babies, assisted suicides, corruption in high places and low places … on and on and on. *Ad nauseam.*

The world is in a mess and if these are not the Last Days I will be amazed. Mind you, it's unlikely that you'll win many friends by saying so: and I don't just mean non-believers. I find in the course of my ministry that enormous numbers of "Christians" refuse to talk about it. They simply do not want even to *think* about it. Maybe something good will turn up! After all, many are telling us that Revival is just around the corner (some would even go so far as to say it's *here*, not that there is much evidence of a transformed society to back up the assertion!). If Revival is truly on God's agenda, folks think, we can relax and wait for *Him* to take the initiative. But that kind of thinking breeds inertia and a withdrawal from mission.

The problem is that the Bible does not encourage a Revival scenario for the Last Days. From a biblical aspect it seems not to be on the Lord's agenda. Quite the reverse. The Bible speaks of major degeneration on all fronts *within* the Church as well as outside it.

In writing of the Last Days in 2 Peter 3:3 Peter wrote, *"First of all, you must understand that in the last days scoffers will come, mocking and following their own evil desires. They will say, 'Where is this "coming" he promised?'"*

That whole chapter, along with 2 Peter 2, makes dramatic and ominous reading. Peter is warning about deception coming into churches, leading unguarded believers astray.

What strikes me is that Peter is so *hard* on the false teachers and false prophets! He is not at all polite towards them: he shows no respect! He certainly doesn't look for signs of good to mitigate the bad and give dubious preachers the benefit of the doubt! The people Peter has in mind are spreading lies about God's Truth and Peter slams them for it with what many observers would call "an appalling lack of love"!

These days we are reluctant to call a spade a spade! We are reluctant to adopt a strict attitude to what we observe as unrighteousness in society, considering such an attitude un-Christian! This is what makes it tough to come to terms with biblical incidents where wickedness is punished. Take, for instance, the attitude of Elijah towards God's enemies, the prophets of Baal (1 Kings 18:40). In the Name of God, Elijah slaughtered them. Then again, there is the remarkable incident recorded in Acts 5 when Ananias and Sapphira were quite literally 'slain in the spirit'. The judgement of God fell on those Church members because they lied to the Holy Spirit. Peter was very much at the centre of that episode and clearly identified with God's action.

We might feel slightly less uncomfortable with the judgement that fell upon the prophets of Baal because they were sworn enemies of God's people, but slaying Ananias and Sapphira just for lying to Him is for many a step too far. Surely God would not do such a thing, would He?

Clearly He did and unless we want to put a blue pencil through that passage and declare it not part of the Bible, we have to accept it as truth.

Just the other day I was struck by an incident at Jericho, when Achan stole things that had been devoted to the Lord. Joshua 7 gives the detail. Here was a situation which some would call justifiable theft. After all, Achan had brought his family through great hardship in the Wilderness, being led by Moses and now by Joshua. Achan and his dependents had very little of this World's goods. As he ran in over the rubble of devastated Jericho Achan spotted a gold ingot and a hoard of silver coins. None of his fellow warriors had spotted them as far as he was aware. But *he* had! What a waste to leave them there! They would guarantee his family's security for generations to come! Further along he came upon a lovely Babylonian cloak, partly buried in the debris. What a gift for his wife, so deprived of nice things! Was this not an obvious blessing from God?

Achan's logic might be acceptable to the World … but it was wholly unacceptable to God. All the members of Achan's family were subsequently killed.

The prophets of Baal were openly defiant, Ananias and Sapphira lied to God and Achan deliberately disobeyed God, choosing to ignore His command through Joshua not to touch any of the spoil. In every case the result was the same: God's judgement fell decisively. The rebels were killed on the spot.

It may be uncomfortable truth, but it *is* truth. These things certainly happened just as they are described. The Lord takes unrighteousness very seriously.

What place does the pursuit of righteousness have in your congregation? What processes are in place to encourage members in a robust and rigorous pursuit of holiness?

But never mind other believers, what place does righteousness have in *my* life? Am I determined to live a holy life, or is my profession of faith simply *religious*?

These biblical incidents, and many others, serve to alert us to the seriousness with which the Lord views our casual approach to faith. It must grieve Him so much. Jesus expressed the heart cry of His Father when He instructed the messenger of the congregation in Laodicea, *"He, the Amen, the Faithful and True Witness, the beginning of the Creation of God, says these things: 'I know your deeds, that you are neither cold nor hot. I wish you were cold or hot. Because you are lukewarm in this way and neither hot nor cold, I am going to spew you out of my mouth ...'"*. That is Revelation 3:14-16.

Then Jesus provides us with the answer in Verse 18. He advises the so-called believers to buy from Him gold purified in the fire (not the slightest trace of dross); to acquire and put on pure white garments (not the vestige of a stain) and to rub in ointment to the eyes to enable uncluttered sight (no hint of visual imperfection).

The use of the words "buy" in the case of gold and clothing and "put on" in the case of eye salve, shows that a positive action is required. Both are active verbs requiring faithful believers to DO something.

How much longer are we to drift along in carefree apostasy: having fallen away from the truth: having spat in the face of God?

The mere fact that I still live and breathe is a mystery of grace. I truly deserve nothing but death and I am still here only because of the mercy of the Lord. Don't ask me to explain 'Why spare me?' because I don't know the answer. All I can say is that He is giving me time to repent and CHANGE. And if I do *not* ... ? Hebrews 10:31 has drifted into my mind: "It is a dreadful thing to fall into the hands of the living God." Make no mistake about it, the writer is addressing *Christians.*

When preaching in a church where I am known I sometimes say, "Dear friends, how much have you changed since I was here last time?" The response is usually broad grins and nervous chuckles, as if to say, "Change? You must be mad!"

But why such incredulity? Is change not the stuff of discipleship? If it is and we are commanded by Jesus to be disciples ourselves and to go and make disciples of others, why are we so thrown by the prospect of change?

It may have something to do with the teaching we have so often been regaled with which states that the Lord God our Father is so loving and kind that He is actually given to indulgence of a kind that turns a blind eye to our sin and iniquity. Righteousness may then be viewed as part of God's character … but not ours.

People who sit through my sermons often say to me, "A great word, Chris!" I accept the praise gratefully (and I trust, humbly), but at the back of my mind there lurks a thought: "So what? I wonder if it will result in *change*?" I'm sure most preachers will feel as I do. I have learned that even rapturous enthusiasm for a sermon means very little. It doesn't impress me any more. What matters is a changed life because *God* has spoken through His Word.

Mind you, I so often do precisely the same thing myself. The Lord speaks! I listen very nicely, then go out and do precisely what *I* want!

It is a pattern repeated regularly through both Israel's history and Church history. That brand of belief is guaranteed to fail because it is the very antithesis of true biblical discipleship.

Chapter Five

On the Watch!

Some words used in Christian circles can be diluted to such a degree that although commonly used they become pretty meaningless. The word 'fellowship' is one such. We use it as a more spiritual alternative to 'Meeting', speaking of the 'Women's Fellowship', the 'Men's Fellowship', the 'Young People's Fellowship' and even 'The Prayer Fellowship'. The word injects a deeper quality into the proceedings, does it not? Well, that's what we suppose!

Then again we speak of having 'good fellowship' when we share cups of tea and biscuits. In fact, 'fellowship' can be used of any and every gathering of believers, whatever their activity! It makes us feel good, friendly, embraced, happy, and accepted.

When you examine the word biblically however you discover something else! Surprise! Surprise! I'm not going to tell you what it is: you can use your concordance to do a word study of *koinonia* for yourself. Look at the way the word is used (for instance) in the Letter to the Philippians. But be prepared for a few shocks!

Have you noticed how the word 'Intercessor' has become fashionable? People who pray for others are being referred to as intercessors.

We use the phrase 'Prayers of Intercession' in our Services to mean praying for the needs of others. That is a proper and necessary activity, but a careful study of intercession in the Bible leads to the conclusion that it goes far beyond going through a list of people and situations we are concerned about. Indeed, it means far more even than committed, regular prayer. Intercession is an extraordinary ministry of 'standing in the gap', whereby the intercessor is very closely identified with the subject of the intercession, sometimes even taking on the burden of the thing prayed about. True intercession can be an agonising business and is not something to be undertaken without a clear leading from the Lord.

Another word that has become fashionable is 'Watchman'. Christians who have an eye for the apocalyptic and are aware of world events are said to have 'A Watchman ministry'. But what is meant by this term?

A century ago there was an amazing amount of interest in the Last Days. Christians were much taken with study of the Scriptures and searching for clues pointing to the Lord's Return, preceding events and events beyond. That search produced a number of interpretations resulting in many different entrenched positions. Quite often those adopting a strong opinion became hyper-critical of believers who thought otherwise, producing division and loss of relationship. Fear of such division has kept some believers well away from prophetic writing concerning the Last Days. They think it safer that way. The best course of action in order to protect our good name and preserve relationship is to ignore contentious issues. Israel being a classic example.

Preachers avoid matters that are considered contentious because they want to preserve their good name as being 'a balanced preacher', never mind what the Bible says!

I am reminded of the wonderful 'Ostrich Song', brought to the world by Michael Flanders and Donald Swann:

"Peek-a-boo, I can't see you: everything must be grand!
Book-a-pee, you can't see me as long as I've got me 'ead in the sand!
Peek-a-boo, it may be true: there's somethin' in what you've said,
But we've got enough troubles in everyday life: I just bury me 'ead!"

Contentious or not, there is so much prophetic writing in the Scriptures concerning the Return of Jesus and the Last Days that we cannot simply put the proverbial 'blue pencil' through it and concentrate on what we consider to be more important truths. If we ignore these prophetic statements of the Bible, we consign enormous chunks to the doubt-bin and leave ourselves in a very vulnerable position. Clearly a dangerous game.

In spite of such general indifference in large numbers of churches, there are many believers who have a renewed desire to know the truth regarding the Return of Jesus and the End Times. Many are poring over the Scriptures to learn all they can. Our Lord's command to "Watch" is being taken seriously. As indeed it should be.

Justification for the idea of being 'Watchmen' is found in passages like Matthew 24:42 and 25:13. In answer to the searching questions of the disciples regarding the fall of Jerusalem (24:3), the sign of Jesus' coming and the end of the age, our Lord gives clear warning.

In regard to the coming siege and fall of Jerusalem He provides stark and instantly recognisable pointers to the Roman invasion and their laying siege to Jerusalem. These were crystal clear warnings intended to be a 'Wake-up call' to alert the believers to the need for immediate escape.

Jesus spoke of the city being surrounded by troops (Luke 21:20) and the erecting of Roman standards on the Temple Mount (Matthew 24:15). These events took place immediately before the terrible events of the 9th of Av in the year AD70. On the evidence of their eyes, the believers obeyed Jesus. They fled the city and crossed the Jordan to enter the mountains at Pella on the far side of the river. *They escaped the conflagration because they took the words of Jesus seriously* (24:16).

So the disciples were prepared for the destruction of Jerusalem by taking seriously the clear pointers provided by Jesus.

However, in the section of His reply in which He answers the question of the disciples regarding the End Times, Jesus is much less precise. Indeed He says that no-one except *the Father* knows about that day or hour (Matthew 24:36, 42-44; 25:13; Luke 12:35-37a).

In contrast to His provision of clues regarding the Roman invasion, He gives no detailed clues at all when speaking of the End Times! He describes how conditions will be, but they are general pointers and not so specific. The single word that shines through as preparing the disciples for the End is *"Watch!"* That is the strong and urgent word that reaches out through the centuries to impact believers today, providing us with Heaven's strategy. *"Watch!"*

But what does our Lord mean when He calls us to *"Watch!"*?

There is a lady in our road who takes 'Neighbourhood Watch' very seriously. She is for ever tweaking the curtains in order to watch the neighbours! She is well aware of what they do and if you give her the chance she will fill your ears with all manner of fascinating bits of information: some of it really juicy! Her watching means that she knows an awful lot about the neighbours!

That is NOT the kind of 'watching' the Lord means! That kind of watching is simply observation to accumulate knowledge. Many believers engage in it: they want to KNOW as much as they can about the Bible, including the Last Things.

But 'watch' as Jesus used the word in Matthew 24 and 25 is *gregoreo* which means 'Be on watch, as a sentry is on watch' – fully alert, trained for battle and ready to engage the enemy.

Paul expresses it well in 1 Corinthians 16:13: *"Watch ye, stand fast in the faith, quit you like men, be strong."*

Keeping watch is more than keeping our eye open! It must impact our studies of the many biblical passages that prophetically describe the Last Things. Supremely the books of Revelation and Daniel and passages like Matthew 24. It is all too easy to treat our subject almost as an academic exercise: simply amassing knowledge.

The call of Jesus takes us much deeper than that. As a determined disciple of Christ I am called to be a sentry: prepared, equipped and poised to wage war. But even more than that – to be *engaged* in war.

Moslems speak of *Jihad*, Holy War. They are at war with the entire non-Moslem world. Even amenable followers of Allah have no choice but to engage their perceived enemies by all means at their disposal.

We can view that with dismay and quite fail to see that our calling is the same! The Islamic understanding of Holy War embraces death and destruction and results in all manner of evil acts. That is the complete opposite of *our* Holy War. As Paul puts it in Ephesians 6:12, *"Our struggle (warfare) is not against flesh and blood."* However, he goes on to describe what our Holy War really is: *"Our struggle is against the rulers, against the authorities, against the powers of this dark world and against the spiritual forces of evil in the heavenly realms."*

This awareness that we are at war all the time is lost on many Christians. But that is the nature of warfare. When Britain was at war with Germany it was not an occasional activity: it was constant. Moment by moment, every day, week in, week out, month by month, year on year … until the victory was declared.

When Jesus described His Church (Matthew 16:18) He said its principal outreach activity was to be all out conflict with the forces of Hell. Throughout His ministry His frequent references to discipleship were shot through with the call to discipline and a life of faith based upon fearless devotion.

Such is the calling of the 'Watchman'. Permanently on the watch, permanently ready for the call to arms, permanently on the *qui vive*, permanently aware of the King's general orders, permanently listening for the King's specific command, permanently watching for enemy activity, consciously ready to use the weapons he has been issued with.

I shall never be off duty this side of the Rapture. Have you ever noticed that in that famous passage in Ephesians 6, the soldier of Christ is not instructed to take the armour *off*? Once on it stays on!

So we are called to be trained, disciplined, determined Watchmen for Christ: engaged in Holy War, committed to training, committed to holiness.

Personal discipline lies at the heart of our warfare. The first battle-front is *me*! If my life is unchanged through my personal submission to God's Word and Spirit, my ability to wage war 'out there' is reduced accordingly. Because I know so much about the Bible and even about the mechanics of spiritual warfare, I can fool myself into thinking that I am mature and able successfully to engage the enemy. Then I wake up! Carnage all around and deep wounds scarring me.

The other day a man said to me, "Those who can, do. Those who cannot, teach. Those who cannot teach, preach!"

I nearly clocked him one! In love of course! But what a perception! No doubt he was pulling my leg, but I was shaken that this might be how some people think. But then again, should I be surprised? As they look at me do they see a genuine soldier of Christ: a man transformed and standing firm?

Food for thought, don't you think?

"Soldiers of Christ arise and put your armour on:
Strong in the strength which God provides through His eternal Son.
Strong in the Lord of Hosts and in His mighty power:
Who in the strength of Jesus trusts is more than conqueror!"

Come along! Let's arise and engage the enemy! I dare you!

(I have written more fully on this vital matter in my book, "Built for Battle!" – see the book list at the end of this volume)

Chapter Six

Back to the Bible!

King Solomon wrote three books in the Hebrew Scriptures: The Song of Songs, Proverbs and Ecclesiastes. Bible teachers say the first he wrote as a young man, the second as a mature man and the third as a reflective older man.

Ecclesiastes is a rather strange book. It is easy to understand, but some of its pronouncements might be considered to be outrageous! Consider 7:28 for example, *"... I found one upright man among a thousand, but not one upright woman among them all!"* That attitude would go down really well these days wouldn't it? Well ...perhaps not!

Mind you, Solomon probably had reasons for his statement. After all, he was surrounded by men involved in his government and had cause to doubt the integrity of many, suspecting them of being in it for their own ends. He had over a thousand women in his life, all vying for his attention, so his observations are informed!

Although written by the King of Israel, Solomon refers to himself with the word *Qoheleth*. It really means "Speaker" as in The Speaker of the House of Commons, an authority figure who presides over debates and carefully weighs arguments. So in Ecclesiastes we have big questions being addressed. What is life really all about? Is there any point to existence? Just look at his opening salvo: *"'Meaningless! Meaningless!' says the Speaker. 'Utterly meaningless! Everything is meaningless.'"*

Why is Solomon expressing such negative opinions? What has happened to this gifted man to whom God had once given divine wisdom, so eloquently expressed in the Book of Proverbs?

The answer may lie partly in Solomon's eye for the ladies! His head had been turned too many times and his foreign wives and concubines had exerted dangerous pressures upon him. Foreign women had brought their foreign gods into Israel and in order to placate them, Solomon had not only built many palaces to accommodate the girls, but many shrines appeared in honour of their gods. Solomon's integrity was sacrificed for sex and his wisdom was compromised. God's wisdom has to be exercised in God's own way or else it becomes something else – certainly not *God's* wisdom.

The King's extraordinary conclusions concerning life's meaninglessness may well stem from his readiness to look for good in false religions and expose himself to too many foreign philosophies and associated literature. In spite of his wisdom he had become thoroughly confused. Where did truth really lie?

The underlying message of Ecclesiastes constitutes a dire warning to God's people against diluting our faith with false notions and permitting a multitude of ideas to pervert the Word of God. Is this how the Lord is addressing us through Solomon's final work?

Many speakers and preachers save a pithy statement for their closing remarks! The idea is that the congregation should leave with something that encapsulates all that has been said but in a concise and memorable form. Solomon is no exception. Consider Ecclesiastes 12:11-14,

"The words of the wise are like goads, their collected sayings like firmly embedded nails – given by one Shepherd. Be warned, my son, of anything in addition to them. **Of making many books there is no end, and much study wearies the body.**
Now all has been heard; here is the conclusion of the matter: fear God and keep His commandments, for this is the whole duty of man. For God will bring every deed into judgment, including every hidden thing, whether it is good or evil."

Having said all, Solomon's conclusion is 'spot-on'. The One New Man Bible renders verse 13b as *"Revere God and keep His commandments: for* **this is the whole man.**" Do I wish to be a "whole man" in God's eyes? A complete man of God, not lacking any good thing? If so, there is a way: *"Revere God and keep His commandments."*

One of the subtle temptations from Solomon's day until our own is to consume masses of books as additional to feeding in *God's* Word. Solomon certainly had access to the Five Books of the Torah, Joshua, Judges, Ruth, many of the Psalms and possibly the Books of Samuel and Job. But I do not believe he was referring to these when he made his observation, *"Of making many books there is no end, and much study wearies the body."* Would it not be extraordinary if he considered study of the books in God's Word to be wearisome to the body!

I must confess that I had always been aware of Ecclesiastes 12:12b but never took it very seriously. In fact it rather amused me by its quaintness. But that is to demean the Word of God. 2 Timothy 3:16 makes it perfectly plain that *"All Scripture is God-breathed and is useful for teaching, rebuking, correcting and training in righteousness, so that the man of God may be perfectly equipped (literally, 'perfect') for every good work."*

I am struck by the similarity between Paul's words and those of Solomon in Ecclesiastes 12:13, *"Revere God and keep His commandments, for this is the whole man"*. (ONMB)

If I have aspirations to be a whole man of God, Solomon's and Paul's words are incontrovertible.

I must confess to being a bibliophile – I love books! I use the word 'confess' deliberately because I believe I am in danger of having a promiscuous relationship with the Bible. There is another literary love in my life – ***BOOKS!***

My bibliophily has given me a hunger for Bible Versions. I have many. Truth to tell, many of them sit on my shelves unread and dusty. But their mere presence has a subtle effect on my mind. I tell myself I *need* lots of versions in order to discover the *true* Truth. "Let's see what the New International Version says. Let's see what the One New Man Bible says. Let's see what the Authorised Version says. Let's see what the New American Standard Version says." Hmmm! Which rendering suits me best?

One of the effects of possessing many translations is that a lot of us never get familiar with any one version and so we have difficulty in quoting the Bible and even *trusting* the Bible.

If too many 'Books' was a problem in Solomon's day, think how he would write today!

The plain, literal meaning of a Bible passage is usually the correct meaning. The Bible speaks for itself. For hundreds of years the Early Church had only the Scriptures as its source of revelation and those believers turned the World right side up.

There then came the dark period prior to the Reformation when for centuries normal believers were reliant upon intermediaries (clergy) who were among the only people who could read. Explaining the meaning of the Bible was the preserve of these intermediaries with multifarious results, depending upon the spiritual state of the preacher!

The Reformation ushered in a period when Bibles appeared in the common languages of Europe and believers were able to read the Word for themselves. So it continued through periods of decline and mighty revival. Most Christians in our land had access to a Bible, even if they did not possess their own copy, so at least those with a hunger for God had the opportunity to feed on His Word.

Today the situation is different. Every one of us has access to a Bible (some to a good dozen or more) and yet most of us are dependent on a class of intermediary to tell us what to believe because apparently we cannot read and understand the Word for ourselves! This class of intermediary is called a "Bible Commentator". Such gifted writers produce a vast range of Bible Commentaries to suit all theological proclivities! I confess to an insatiable hunger for Commentaries!

Here's how it works. I read a portion of Scripture. I ask the Lord to make His message plain. After a moment's hurried thought I reach for a Commentary to see what the writer has to say. This stimulates me to see the passage from *his* point of view, then I simply acknowledge it and pass on to the next verse for a repeat operation. Either that or I turn to a *second* Commentary or even a *third* until I come to an interpretation that suits me. The subtlety in this is that I have replaced Bible Study with Commentary Study.

Then there are biographies, theological volumes, inspirational books … the list seems endless! They populate our bookshelves, litter our bedside cabinets, they accompany us on our travels and make useful gifts. Aren't they wonderful? I've produced a good many myself, so I'm somewhat biased!

But what is the effect of these books? Is it lasting or temporary? Do they impact me to make me a better disciple? Really and truly? Or is it wishful thinking?

Have you observed the way in which many Christian bookshop-keepers have altered the description of their premises? What were formerly "Bible bookshops" have become "*Christian* bookshops" and the change within is as revealing as the facade. In many the Bibles no longer occupy the prominent place they once did. This is now taken by "inspirational books" while the Bibles are relegated to the rear of the shop.

That development can be equally reflected in our *personal* choices?

Let me ask a question. If you compare the amount of time you spend in a week reading "good Christian books" with the amount of time you spend feeding in the Scriptures, how does the comparison look?

Where has this somewhat cavalier attitude to the Bible led us? Up the creek without a paddle in many cases! There are churches where the Bible is virtually replaced with dumbed down, trendy alternatives in the mistaken (and devil inspired) belief that the Bible as it is, is far too difficult for the vast majority of believers to understand!

WHO ARE THEY KIDDING?

If our forebears were able to be radiant Christians armed with only a Bible, what is the matter with *us*? Recent decades have surely proved that adopting a casual attitude to Scripture is taking us nowhere. How many believers do we know who are valiant for truth and truly alive in the Spirit. How much true New Testament power is on display in Britain today? Precious little, sadly.

Please don't think I have become a bibliophobe in my old age! I am not *against* books, but I honestly believe they have taken the place of the Bible in many cases. That is what I fear. So what should we do? I suggest the following:

1)   Do NOT take your "good Christian books" (or CDs and DVDs) and burn them! Many of them have their uses just so long as they are kept in their place, and that place must be subservient to the Bible itself.

2)   Decide upon a good translation (take advice if you need to) making sure it *is* a translation and not a paraphrase (there's a big difference). And then STICK to it.

3)   For an experimental period of a whole month, keep all Christian books at bay by shutting them in a cupboard. Lock the cupboard and give the key to someone else for safe keeping! I'm being serious. The effect on you will tell you a lot!

4) Spend the month reading and studying ONLY the Scriptures: allowing the Bible to be its own commentator and interpreter.

5) After the month is over, be honest with yourself and ask how much you have been wonderfully blessed through your exposure to the unadulterated Word of God! It might just change your whole life!

6) When you take your books out again, treat them cautiously! They represent a great danger, so please do not slither back into the old habits!

Why not give it a try? Go on – it could transform your life!

Chapter Seven

Preach it, brother!

Preachers are privileged people. They are called to speak to people as from our Father God and this solemn calling must be treated with the utmost seriousness by the one who speaks and also by those who hear.

When I was born my parents decided to give me the name 'Christopher'. It is not a name that features on either branch of my Family Tree, but my godly parents were quite convinced that this should be my name. The name has a Greek origin and means "Christ carrier". Not a bad choice of name for a man who would become a preacher of the gospel!

After my New Birth at the age of 17, I found myself gravitating towards those people who loved the Bible. As I have said before, one of my inspirations in those early years (and ever since) was Dr. Martyn Lloyd-Jones, whose preaching absolutely gripped me! The first time I heard him was in a country town in Somerset to which he had been invited. The power of his preaching pinned me to my pew! It was not only his masterful delivery it was also the authority with which he spoke. I would describe it as truly the Word of the Lord made alive under the anointing of the Holy Spirit.

I became a student at Tyndale Hall Theological College in Bristol at the age of 25. In various ways the Lord confirmed the direction of my ministry as a preacher. A fellow student (who later became Bishop of Mount Kenya East) had a personal word of encouragement for me in the form of a Puritan quote. It read, *"Thou art a preacher of the Word ... mind thy business!"* Forty eight years on that quotation still adorns my Study wall and every morning it focuses the mind dramatically!

The Lord was so good to take me to Tyndale Hall for four tremendous, formative years, because the Tyndale Faculty was devoted to preparing men in the Reformed Evangelical tradition: that means the Bible and the Sovereignty of God were unswervingly central to our training.

When I left College to be Ordained, my then College Principal gave me a book. In it he inscribed, *"Preach the Word; be urgent ..."*. Only five words from 2 Timothy 4, but you will appreciate how they impacted me and helped to confirm what I believed to be the 'burden' the Lord had put in my heart. I knew I must be a preacher.

Over the years I have read a number of books that sought to encourage effective preaching, but one stands in a league of its own. It was published in 1971: *"Preaching and preachers"* by Dr. Martyn Lloyd-Jones. An insightful book that is intensely practical. When people ask me about preaching, I simply reply, "Go and consult 'The Doctor'!"

But for even greater insight into the nature and execution of preaching I turn to the Scriptures themselves. There surely we find encouragement enough as we study the ministry of the Bible prophets and preachers.

One of the most helpful contributions is Paul's exhortation referred to above: namely, 2 Timothy 4:1-5. The full text in the 'One New Man Bible' reads,

"I am charging you before God and Messiah Jesus, the One who is going to judge the living and the dead, at His appearance and in His Kingdom: you must now preach the Word, you must now be ready in season, out of season, you must now correct, you must now rebuke, you must now encourage, with great patience and every kind of instruction. For there will be a time when sound teaching will not be listened to but they will heap up teachings according to their own desires in themselves, what their ears are itching to hear and indeed they will turn their ears from the truth, and they will turn aside to myths. But you must continually be sober in everything, you must now bear hardship patiently, you must now do the work of an evangelist, you must now fulfil your ministry."

As Timothy read those words his mind must have exploded with the realization that he was being confronted with awesome revelation from Heaven! If Timothy had any concept of what his calling was before Paul's remarks, he certainly knew it afterwards! The thing was awesome to contemplate, elevating the preaching of the Word to exalted heights. Timothy must have been completely floored by the hugeness of his commission.

In 2 Timothy 3:16 Paul had just written that all Scripture is God-inspired, and it is these very Scriptures that enable a man of God to meet all demands because they equip him for *every* good work. Think of that … and marvel at the grace of God in giving such a tool to His servants!

In order to show Timothy the extraordinary nature of his calling Paul sets it in a dramatic context, speaking of days to come when men would no longer put up with sound doctrine but go after those whose preaching suited their own proclivities, even turning away from the Truth and embracing all manner of mythical nonsense supposing it to be Truth.

When is this time Paul has in mind? In the first instance, 2 Timothy 4:3 must surely refer to a time Timothy could relate to: a time in his near future when Timothy's own preaching would fall on deaf ears. Those are wrong who view the Early Church as being flawless! It was far from that! Falling away from the Truth set in within a short space of time following the Pentecost outpouring. Paul's great letters bristle with strong rebuke concerning error in the churches and the second and third chapters in the Apocalypse of John contain letters to the churches that demonstrate a general falling away from the truth *at the time* and well before the end of the First Century!

In 2 Thessalonians 2:3 Paul also speaks of a falling away. But here he sets it in the context of the End Times. Paul is envisioning the falling away accompanying the emergence of the "man of lawlessness" – the Antichrist. So Paul is being truly prophetic here. He sees a soon fulfilment and also a further and greater fulfilment in the future when the Antichrist appears. An end-time falling away from the Truth will come about in preparation for the arrival of Antichrist on the world stage. These are twin events to signal the approach of the Last Days.

So who is it that will fall away from the truth? Logically those who have once been *firm and secure* in the truth. In other words, Bible believing Christians! If these are *not* the ones described, the concept of falling away from the Truth makes no sense.

Does this mean that some who lay claim to be 'Evangelical' will abandon the truths of the gospel through pressures let loose in the time of the End? Presumably yes. Does it mean they will lose their salvation? Not if they were truly born again: but tragically they will lose their reward in the coming Kingdom.

The context of Paul's injunction to Timothy makes plain the Lord's countermeasure to the problem. Preaching! Modern opinion tends to relegate preaching to the sidelines and in its place provide trendier means of proclaiming God's Word. But if we take Scripture as our guide, it is clear that preaching is God's preferred method. Nearly every major Bible character was a preacher. Preachers proclaimed the Kingdom of God; preachers established the Church; preachers declaimed the truth of Christ before hostile leaders and crowds. And yet today there is a widespread desire to see preaching banished from the life of the Church and the nation in favour of dumbed-down alternatives. But if we may say that preaching is the primary Bible way of communicating God's Word by the Spirit, by what authority do we deprecate it? Perhaps this is a ploy of the devil in his attempt to make the Church impotent and incapable of defending itself against the forces of evil, let alone defeating them.

As you read my selected translation of 2 Timothy 4:2, you will have noted the use of the word *"now"*. The 'One New Man Bible' uses the word to indicate the Aorist Tense of the Greek verbs. It requires this crucial emphasis: *NOW!* The urgency in Paul's appeal is obvious. As we consider his call to preach we need to make a firm resolve to get on with it, affront or please!

Being ready *"in season and out of season"* provides no time off! We are constantly on duty, so to speak. The ministry of a preacher is not limited to the time he spends in the pulpit: he is called to declare God's Word in any and every situation whether people listen to him or not. As Paul comments in Romans 10:14-15, *"How then shall they call on Him in whom they have not believed? And how shall they believe in Him of whom they have not heard? And **how shall they hear without a preacher**? And how shall they preach except they be sent? As it is written, 'How beautiful are the feet of them that preach the gospel of peace and bring glad tidings of good things!'"* (King James Version)

In 2 Timothy 4:2 Paul uses several words to show the impact that Timothy's preaching must have. Paul uses *elegcho*, meaning 'reprove or correct', indicating that personal discipline in righteous living is primary. This is confirmed with the word *epitimao*, meaning 'rebuke', a very unpopular thing to do! To rebuke is to tell people to STOP what they are doing and to stop it NOW! Hardly a guarantee of becoming a popular preacher!

Parakaleo is a much more welcome term meaning 'exhort and encourage'. It carries with it the idea of coming alongside people with positive, loving care: providing direction towards fulfilment and success.

Timothy is told that all of this must be done *"with all longsuffering and doctrine"* (KJV). Infinite patience with the people matched by the impartation of clear biblical truth is the requirement. There is balance here that is very winsome but it is no light undertaking. Remember my Puritan quote: *"Thou art a preacher of the Word ... mind thy business!"*

Paul's deliberate choice of words demonstrates the massive impact of true preaching in the power of the Holy Spirit. Under God it has the power to change lives but it requires the willingness of the preacher to 'stick his head above the parapet' and take the terrible risk of rejection and hostility.

Paul's projection into the future in verses 3-4 was obviously going to prove true in Timothy's day, but, if anything, his words have even greater resonance for us in our own. Sound doctrine is not on the agenda of increasing numbers of churches. Experiences, yes: sound doctrine, no!

In the light of Paul's warning it should come as no surprise that preaching has faded from the priority list of many believers. It needs to be returned to its rightful place. But not preaching for preaching's sake. The whole point is that when suffering really hits, it is only the solid foundation of our faith that will keep us standing.

The challenge to me as to every preacher is to speak God's Truth, the whole of God's Truth and nothing but God's Truth. I have the sense that the Holy Spirit is taking *me* in hand. He is asking for a solemn review of my ministry. He is saying what He has actually been saying since I was 17 years old: "Go on … preach the Word … I *dare* you!"

Chapter Eight

Church on the march!

In the days of the New Testament, the *Via Maris* snaked across Israel and up through the Golan Heights to Damascus and beyond. It was a hugely important trunk road and through the centuries carried hundreds of thousands of travellers of every kind. To the south it penetrated Egypt and to the east it stretched beyond Mesopotamia to connect with the Spice Route and the Silk Road from the distant Orient.

Traders, travellers and troops all tramped the *Via Maris* and at least two of them left indelible footprints as they journeyed.

Saul of Tarsus trod the road with purposeful tread as he headed for Damascus, determined to stamp out a disgusting and blasphemous movement that sought to undermine his precious religion, pretending that God had become a man! This abomination had to be crushed and Saul believed himself the man to do it. Armed with credentials with the High Priest's imprimatur fixed to them, he set his face for Damascus and was approaching the city when his life was totally shattered and transformed. Jesus met him (For a brief, yet detailed account of Paul's life, see my booklet "Saul of Tarsus").

Some time before, another powerful man, Peter, had been confronted by Jesus on the same road. The encounter is described by Matthew and Mark in their gospel accounts.

As it ascends from the Jordan Valley, the *Via Maris* crosses the Golan Heights in the shadow of Mount Hermon. In Jesus' day it passed through a major Roman town that had an ancient and chequered past.

The Old Testament knows the site as Baal Hermon (Judges 3:3, 1 Chronicles 5:23), telling us its location in the foothills of the great mountain and also indicating the activities for which the place became notorious: Baal worship.

The worship of Baal was a terrible business. Baal was the storm God of the Canaanites and when lightning flashed and thunder crashed, Baal was speaking and making his vile demands upon his worshippers. These included child sacrifice. Mothers deliberately driven insane with drugs were persuaded by devilish priests and prophets to offer up their little ones to appease Baal and they did it.

Baal's consort was the goddess Asherah. Worshipping her involved all manner of sexual depravity because she was the fertility goddess.

Blend the two religions and you get an idea of the goings on through the ages at Baal Hermon. Multiple layers of evil providing a haunt for demons.

The arrival of the Greeks saw major development at Baal Hermon. A great artesian spring spewed from the bowels of the earth and through a huge cavern at the base of the rockface. The cavern was known to local people as 'The Gates of Hell'. Acknowledging the spiritual powers in the place, the Greeks built a temple to Zeus and believed it the birthplace of the god Pan, renaming it Panyas.

Enter the Romans. They were impressed by the esoteric character of the place and wanting to assert their supremacy they built a temple in honour of Jupiter, thereby over-stamping his evil sovereignty on the site.

Cue Herod the Great! When he died his Kingdom was divided by Rome into regions ruled by his sons. The Golan came under the rule of Herod Philip. Wishing to ingratiate himself with the occupying Romans, Philip put up a temple in honour of the Emperor and renamed the city, Caesarea Philippi, in order to honour Caesar … and himself!

It is to this city that Jesus came with His disciples as he travelled towards the heights of Mount Hermon, there to be transfigured (Matthew 16:13-17:13).

Matthew 16:13 tells us that as they approached Caesarea Philippi, Jesus asked His disciples, *"Who do you say I am?"*

The question takes on huge implications when we remember *where* it was asked. So much evil had soaked into the place down the centuries that we might expect our

Lord to avoid it. But it is as if He asked His question quite deliberately within the setting of such an evil environment. Here surely is an encouragement for those of us who sense that an evil environment inhibits or even prohibits revelation of Jesus through us! It simply is not true.

In response to Jesus it is Peter who ventures to speak. It is a moment when heaven breaks through the veil and as he opens his mouth pure revelation pours out: *"You are the Messiah, the Son of the living God."*

That revelation provides the rock upon which Jesus would build His church, investing it with such power and authority that the combined powers of hell would not overcome it or be able to resist it.

Such is the immensity of the revelation and it should make a shattering impact upon us. Jesus is saying that His church is invincible.

"Pull the other one!" I hear you protest. "What nonsense! Just look at us: a pathetic, powerless imitation of Church – the butt of the nation's jokes. Invincible, indeed!"

Well, either Jesus was speaking nonsense or else we have to reassess our position.

The key issue is, "Whose Church is it anyway?" Significantly the exact quote of Jesus is, *"I will build MY Church"*. Its foundation is Jesus Himself: the Messiah: the King of Kings, the Great High Priest, God the Son.

Jesus is saying, "I want My Church back! I want My Word to rule. Allow My prophetic Word to illuminate your understanding of what is happening all around you. Wake up! Yes, it is true, My Church is invincible: but only MY CHURCH!"

I very much doubt if the setting in which any of us finds himself is remotely like Caesarea Philippi when Jesus was there. However dark our situation it cannot hold a candle to that awful place. So if heaven can reveal the profound truth about Jesus *there,* heaven can surely reveal Jesus through us in *our* situation. The key is to have the courage to open our mouths in order for heaven to speak out through them.

The contrast between the authority of Jesus' true Church and that of the Church we see today is stark. It is all too easy to be critical of every church but our own! But the fact remains that however successful we think our church is, it falls far short of the simple statement made by Jesus: *"The authorities of Hell shall not be able to overcome it (or hold out against it)".* This is the literal meaning of Matthew 16:18.

The only time when we come anywhere close to such a situation is in time of revival and renewal. Many of our readers will look back wistfully to the sixties and seventies to the *early* Charismatic Renewal, when healing and deliverance were taking place and many people were being born again.

The question asked is, "Why is this not happening today?" It is followed by a supplementary one, "Clearly the Lord has not changed, so isn't it obvious that the fault must be with us?"

That sounds right. It *must* be right … mustn't it? But if it is as simple as that, we would be forced to conclude that in the period leading up to the Outpouring, believers were far more holy than we are now! Is that true? Not if *my* memory serves! It was not the result of our deserving, but entirely a matter of grace. God moved sovereignly which meant we were able to do here what had been decreed by heaven! We saw it for ourselves. It was a demonstration of Matthew 16:19!

Jesus said, *"Whatever you bind on earth will have been bound in heaven, and whatever you loose on earth will have been loosed in heaven!"* This is the correct translation of His words.

But note the implication. The Church that Jesus builds has authority *only* to implement on earth what has *already* been decreed in heaven.

In that verse we read that concerning His Church Jesus declared, *"I will give you the keys of the kingdom of heaven."* Surprisingly the "you" there is singular, so Jesus is addressing Peter, the pioneering evangelist, who would be the first to unlock the kingdom to those who should be saved. Millions of witnesses and evangelists would follow in that glorious ministry! Hallelujah!

Do we not long to see the Lord moving through us? Are we eaten up with frustration as we see the onward march of Islam and the seeming inability of churches and governments to act? Do we despair at the appalling ignorance of so many Evangelicals in regard to God's purposes for Israel? Are we trembling as we see anti-Semitism rearing its demonic head in Europe and in every continent?

Do we feel impotent in the face of the current evils let loose?

Is the solution that you and I should get our act together? Is it down to us? It seems to me that the answer must be "Yes", but by itself that is *not* the answer.

If Matthew 16:19 is an accurate translation of our Lord's words, we can only see answers to prayer and success in ministry *when heaven sanctions it.* We are desperate for a sovereign move of God. That is the prior need. We are confronted with the awesome truth that God is God. If He does not move sovereignly, nothing of the true life of heaven can break through here.

It was revelation of the glory of Jesus that initiated His pronouncements regarding His Church. It was revelation of the glory of Jesus that initiated the ministry of Paul. At the heart of Daniel's prophecies was revelation of the glory of Jesus (Daniel 10:4-10). It was revelation of the glory of Jesus that was the catalyst in the situation that faced John on the Island of Patmos (Revelation 1:9-18).

Our longing to see change in our personal relationship with Jesus and our desperate yearning to see the outpouring of God's power upon the Church must surely start right here as we cry out to God for revelation of His dear Son: falling before Him in desolation and repentance. Surely He is the God who responds to the heart cry of His people. But I need to understand that without Him I can do nothing. That applies to my ministry, but more particularly it applies to *me*. I will never change unless the Holy Spirit first moves in my life. It must be His initiative to which I respond in faith: not the other way round.

The revelation of Jesus to Daniel left him prostrate before Him. So it was for Paul. So it was for John. So it is when a vision of the glorious Saviour is granted to *us*. Isaiah was undone when he saw the Lord (Isaiah 6:1-5): the experience exposed him completely, but the consequences for him were glorious

In our chapel on Sunday morning Jim, our preacher, spoke on Revelation 2:4. He spoke about loss of our first love. We all sat there, challenged and resentful that he should put his finger on the issue and spoil our lunch! But then he said this: "Do I really *want* to have my first love for Jesus restored?"

For the Ephesian church, addressed by the Lord, the answer was repentance (Revelation 2:5). As we assess where our rebellion has got us, we need to repent: to come to our senses and return to the Lord Himself: falling before Him and staying there until He raises us up.

OK, so we have a life to live and a ministry to fulfil. But as I once heard a preacher say, "Am I so taken up with the work of the Lord that I have neglected the Lord of the work?"

It's high time I fell on my face before the Lord in order to pour out my repentance and by His grace to recover my first love for Him. That's far more important than exercising my ministry!

Perhaps it's time for me to give up standing before the people and to start falling before the Lord!

What do you think about *you*? Is it time for action?

YES, IT IS!

Chapter Nine

The weight is over … here's hoping!

People reckon that moving house is one of the most stressful things you can undertake. I believe it! Lindy and I are in the throes of a move and it's grim. We're hoping to move to a much more expensive part of the country so our available funds won't stretch to a straight swap. We need to "down-size", as they say.

This word strikes dread into my heart. In order to down-size I need to … down-size! To get rid of everything that simply will not fit into the new house. Is this a terrible prospect, or is it a terrible prospect? For me it is not only terrible, it is simply frightful, odious and loathsome! I'm having to off-load so many books, study notes, clothes and cherished clutter … and all in the name of "LIVING LIGHT".

That's what Lindy calls it and I shudder every time it's repeated: "Darling, we have to live light; we have to live light …!"

OK, so I'm getting the message and hating every syllable of it. But I know she's right. It's quite gutting, but my beloved usually *is* right! So farewell, cherished old friends and hello, builders' skip!

As I am writing this, a scene shift comes to mind. I'm picturing a packed Roman stadium with a line of contestants preparing to hurtle down the running track in a bid to achieve the laurel crown.

It is fascinating to find such a scene described in Hebrews *12:1-3*:

"Therefore, since we are surrounded by such a great cloud of witnesses, let us throw off everything that hinders and the sin that so easily entangles, and let us run with perseverance the race marked out for us. Let us fix our eyes on Jesus, the pioneer and perfecter of our faith, who for the joy set before Him endured the cross, scorning its shame, and sat down at the right hand of the throne of God. Consider Him who endured such opposition from sinful men, so that you will not grow weary and lose heart."

This description of a sports event is graphic. And it is surprising when we remember that the writer is a first century Jew writing for Jews. How come he knows so much about the Games? No self respecting Jew would be seen inside a Roman stadium. In order to compete the athletes ran naked. Perfectly scandalous to a Jew. Then again, the Games were dedicated to Greek and Roman gods. This too prevented Jewish participation, even as spectators.

The writer's knowledge can only be based upon street talk. In Hebrews 13:24 he describes *"those from Italy"* who send the readers their greetings. This may mean that the letter was sent from Rome. It would be difficult to live in Rome (or any of the provincial cities for that matter) and not be aware of Rome's obsession with sport. The excited conversations that took place on the street would have given Jewish people detailed knowledge of what went on behind those closed gates even though they would never experience it for themselves. Doubtless they knew the names of great competing athletes and rubbed shoulders with thousands of spectators who gave first hand accounts of the stirring spectacle.

The writer describes a *"great cloud of witnesses"*. Some modern translations prefer the word "crowd". But they are wrong. The word "cloud" is a deliberate choice because it so well describes the scene from the athlete's point of view. There he is, poised at the starting line with every muscle tense in anticipation of the starting signal. His eyes are fixed on the finishing tape. To deviate even for a split second will result in failure and defeat. He can hear the mounting roar of the crowd massed on the terraces, but he cannot see them clearly: his focus is fixed on the tape. The individuals in that enormous crowd appear to him simply as a blur – a cloud!

This dramatic spectacle provides the writer of Hebrews with a most wonderful encouragement for believers facing great challenge and hardship. It has resonated with believers through the running centuries and certainly resonates with me!

Our writer depicts faith that overcomes as if it were a great race. All the participants in the Games are determined to succeed and are 100% committed. There is no other way. They are trained through personal discipline and each is brought to supreme fitness by his trainer. All become supremely fit but in addition each individual athlete is prepared meticulously for his own event and the regime differs between disciplines. A sprinter is prepared quite differently from a discus thrower, needing certain muscles to be highly developed because of the particular demands of his event.

The trainer is skilled to recognise the potential in each athlete, analysing muscle structure and aptitude and then applying a rigid training programme in order to produce the very best result.

All of this speaks volumes about my race of faith and it too requires a very high standard of *spiritual* fitness. This is where I start screaming for mercy! I do not want to apply myself to the rigours of training! Give me the quiet life please: let me relax in the welcome embrace of religion and feed on whatever delicacies tickle my spiritual tastebuds!

I hope you are getting the message here. High performance discipleship requires total dedication to the Trainer's manual of discipline and His training regime. We're talking Scripture here and the rigorous application of the Word by the power and leading of the Holy Spirit.

The Holy Spirit knows the direction of my life and the nature of my true ministry and so He sees to it that I am developing the particular gifts I need in order to function to the best of my ability. It's very exciting.

For me it was driven home by an African friend when we were at College together. I referred to it earlier. David Gitari gave me a Puritan quote that still stares down at me from my Study wall: "Thou art a preacher of the Word – Mind thy business!" Concise and to the point!

This question of being content to apply myself to my personal calling is one that the apostles faced. In John 21 we find Peter being commissioned by Jesus. It is a most amazing passage. Jesus is highlighting Peter's distinctive calling: *"Feed my lambs; feed my sheep."* How precious is that?

Yet Peter immediately bursts out as he catches a glimpse of the disciple whom Jesus loved, *"Lord, what about **him**?"*

Our Lord's reply shows His exasperation. *"If I want him to remain alive until I return, what is that to you?* ***You must follow me.****"*

In other words, "Peter, get on with your own ministry: I'll take care of your brother's".

In Hebrews 11 our writer has described an astonishing cavalcade of former athletes who have successfully competed in the faith race. Men and women of the Scriptures who have persevered in faith against incredible odds and have come thundering through in victory. These are the witnesses who have lived the truth, the whole truth and nothing but the truth. Their testimony is the inspiration for the runners to give them heart. Their cheers ring through the centuries: "Go on! Go on! You can do it! We did it and so can you! Keep running! You'll get to the end and when you do, you'll have no regrets! That's a PROMISE! Praise the Lord!"

One of the essentials in running a race is to be focused on the right spot. The finishing tape must be in the centre of the athlete's focus and as he runs he homes in on that, with no diverting glance to right or left.

For us, the goal is Jesus Himself. Our eyes are fixed there with no diverting glances. So often Church affairs become our focus and Jesus slips from our vision. The inevitable result is failure and defeat. Take the example of Peter stepping out of the boat on the Sea of Galilee. Matthew 14:22-33 describes the incident. No sooner were Peter's eyes diverted from the face of Jesus onto the wind and the waves than he began to sink!

Fixing my eyes on Jesus requires a determined focus upon Him as I discover Him in the Scriptures. To be absorbed in revelation of Him in the New Testament and through prophecy and type in the Hebrew *Tanakh* is the heart of victorious faith.

The KJV rendering of Hebrews 12:1 is *"let us lay aside every weight."*

This is where it gets up close and personal! The word *weight* is the Greek *ogkon*. It is used in classical literature for excessive physical weight. Obesity comes close! The picture here is of an aspiring athlete who is overweight. Such a person has no chance to be a successful runner. He has a weight problem. He has excessive fat acquired through over indulgence, eating the wrong things and lack of exercise. He has no chance of competing in the Games in any serious fashion.

Excess weight lies under the skin. It is internal: an inner hindrance to success that must be dealt with in a rigorous manner. No excuses, no half measures, just disciplined hard graft. That is the price of success.

When the writer uses this word *ogkon* it suggests hindrances that lie inside us. We might include personal failings and weaknesses that impede our faith. Pride, anger, lust, envy, resentment ... these are real problems that lie hidden within but which have devastating impact on our discipleship.

No athlete competing in the Greek or Roman Games could possibly get away with indulging in *ogkon*. Nor can we. We must put it to death, as Paul urges in Colossians 3:5.

Hebrews 12:1 goes on to refer to *"the sin that so easily entangles."*

Here is something *external* that can have an equally devastating effect upon performance. The picture that suggests itself is of an athlete wrapped in a Roman toga and attempting to run! He would quickly end up on his nose with the stands rocking with laughter! Athletes were stripped for action to allow maximum freedom to their limbs. Greek and Roman runners ran naked but it was not for salacious purposes: it was to maximise performance on the track. Athletes today wear as little as possible in order to have freedom of movement.

The whole point being made by the writer is that in order to be successful in the most important event of our lives – the race of faith – we need as little clutter as possible. Anything we pick up that is inappropriate to our running simply must be thrown away. Possessions, relationships, habits, activities ... all must be reassessed. Do I *need* this? Is this helping or hindering my training?

Off-loading is a rotten business. *I know*! We're right in the middle of this challenge with regard to the move, but I also know that off-loading everything that hinders my spiritual life is an even greater challenge.

But here's the thing: I **HAVE** TO DO IT. Do I *want* to? No I do not! I hate the very thought of it. But I have to get on with it and stop whinging.

"Lord, please help me to get serious about this and discard *everything* that hinders my progress and thwarts my maturing. Even if it means dropping valued relationships and activities and ridding myself of the television!"

I certainly need all the grace I can get to put this into effect and keep it effective.

As I have developed this article a thought has been growing. To live light has a much deeper connotation. My Saviour is the Light of the world and He has told me to be the Light of the world (John 8:12 and Matthew 5:14) and through His indwelling Holy Spirit Jesus shines through me as I live exclusively for Him.

That surely is the highest accolade any person can receive: "I see Jesus Christ in him". "To encounter him is to encounter Jesus!"

Go on! Live Light! Let it shine!

(See further my booklet, "Going for Gold")

Chapter Ten

"Do I go … or do I stay?"

It was surely going to attract large numbers of Christians. The banner headline describing the convention was 'Voice of the Final Generation'. I was thrilled to be involved, not least because of the courage shown in selecting such a title. It demonstrated the settled view of the organisers that
1) We are the Final Generation before the Lord returns and
2) We have to use our voice to shout the warning.

Surely the organisers could expect a massive attendance. After all, these are clearly the Last Days in the final run up to our Lord's return and we believers need to be thoroughly prepared to face coming suffering as the precursor to the glory that will be ours. Furthermore we need to be strengthened in our commitment to shout the alarm to those in our churches and to people out in the world.

I certainly expected that certain 'Christians' would avoid such an event: those who are nominal or of a timid disposition or entrenched in tradition for whom talk of the Last Days is irrelevant to their brand of 'Church'. But what truly shocked me was that the attendance was so low from Christians with a name for being Evangelical and Pentecostal. True, there were *some* there: but so *few*. Furthermore it was tragic to see that hardly any of the local

Pastors/Ministers/Vicars put in an appearance! It was as if they were boycotting the event and discouraging their people from attending. It may not be so, but that is certainly how it appeared.

Was it fear? Was it indifference? Or was it another symptom that many of us are falling away from the truth?

Why in many churches is so little preached about the imminent return of Jesus? Why do we seldom hear about imminent suffering for Christ and ways in which we can prepare for it and stand in it? We appear to be falling away from the tough truth in the Bible and opting rather for 'smooth things'. The sorts of thing Paul warned about in Romans 16:18 when he said they led to deception. Isaiah wrote of God's people and described them as children unwilling to listen to the Lord's instruction -
"They say to the seers, 'See no more visions!' and to the prophets, 'Give us no more visions of what is right! Tell us pleasant things, prophesy illusions. Leave this way, get off this path, and stop confronting us with the Holy One of Israel.'" (Isaiah 30:10-11)

Choosing to opt for anything less than the full revelation of the Bible is apostasy: falling away from the Truth. I used to think that the 'apostate Church' was still a long way down the road. I did not understand I was embroiled in it. Then I woke up! It's here.

Anything contrary to the Lord's Word is an expression of apostasy. Any teaching given by a church that does not accord with the Bible is apostate. To the degree that a church takes a non-biblical stand on doctrine and lifestyle, it is apostate. This surrounds us and is becoming clearer every day.

The word 'apostasy' is the English form of the Greek word *'apostasia',* falling away. My English dictionary says it means 'abandonment of one's religious principles; a revolt from ecclesiastical obedience'. So an apostate is a renegade.

The word appears in 2 Thessalonians 2:3, where Paul writes of the coming day of the Lord,
"Don't let anyone deceive you in any way, for that day will not come until the apostasy occurs and the man of lawlessness is revealed."

Paul refers to two things that will happen in the world before Jesus comes again. Something terrible will occur in the Church that coincides with the emergence of the man of lawlessness, referred to in the letters of John as "Antichrist" (1 John 2:18, 22; 4:3 and 2 John 1:7). The terrible thing that will occur in the Church is apostasy which is now all around us, suggesting that the Antichrist is on the threshold of world domination. He is presumably already here readying himself, and he stands poised to step onto the world's stage. It would need exceedingly blinkered vision not to see that falling away from the Truth is now endemic.

Economic disaster appears to be worldwide although the powers that be do their best to hide it from us and none of them appears to have the wit to halt the collapse. This is matched by the collapse of all the pillars in our society. Nothing is secure and peace is a rare commodity. So the scene is being set for Antichrist to declare his promise of peace and restored prosperity if only our leaders will give him the necessary and absolute authority to act. We're all being softened up for that moment and it cannot be far away.

For many years I have sought to be a man of peace. I have shared my misgivings privately but I have resisted the (often powerful) urge to shout the warning. Now the defining moment has come and it's time to shout. *'Come out from among them and be separate!'*

That command appears in Paul's second letter to Corinth. He is telling the believers not to be yoked together with unbelievers. Here is 2 Corinthians 6:14-7:1,
"Do not be yoked together with unbelievers. For what do righteousness and wickedness have in common? Or what fellowship can light have with darkness? What harmony is there between Christ and lawlessness? What does a believer have in common with an unbeliever? What agreement is there between the temple of God and idols? For we are the temple of the living God. As God has said, 'I will live with them and walk among them, and I will be their God and they will be My people. Therefore come out from among them and be separate', says the Lord. 'Touch no unclean thing and I will receive you. I will be a Father to you and you will be my sons and daughters', says the Lord Almighty.

Since we have these promises, dear friends, let us purify ourselves from everything that contaminates body and spirit, perfecting holiness out of reverence for God."

We live among the people of the world but with totally different values and power – *God's* power. Some of Jesus' disciples through the years have had to pay a high price for doing that because the world *hates* them. Such disciples have never opted out and removed themselves from the world, but thousands have been (and are being) *driven* out, imprisoned and even killed.

This is an uncomfortable and inconvenient truth that has impact upon our attitude to the churches we attend. If we are required by our church leaders to believe certain things that are unscriptural or to tolerate and even indulge ways of life that are clearly opposing God's standards, we cannot stand idly by without speaking out and acting positively. We are responsible before the Lord for our own spiritual state.

There are, of course, many differences between denominations and even individual churches that do not constitute matters of essential doctrine. But where Scripture is compromised in terms of belief or life style we have to think hard and change direction. In taking a strong stand we run risks of being accused of 'rocking the boat', but we must (as Peter put it) obey God rather than men, whatever the personal cost (Acts 5:29).

Submitting to the authority of church leaders is plainly required, but only as long as they themselves are submitting to the authority of Scripture. Leaders violate their position of authority when they fail to lead according to the Bible.

It is my personal view that we should stay in our churches for as long as we can, seeking to maintain love and truth, allowing the holiness and love of Jesus to shine through us. We identify with all we can, but avoid anything that does not agree with the Bible, in matters of belief or practice. We must avoid it like the plague from now on.

To take such a stand – especially when we go public about it – is to invite misunderstanding both from leaders and congregations. No one likes to be criticised, and questioning doctrinal standpoints and lifestyle choices can be extremely provocative. Such questioning should always be done with grace and love, but that does not mean it must be avoided or done in fear. 'Speaking the truth' must always be done in love, but true love means 'speaking the truth'! To point out where fellow believers and leaders are astray from the Bible is an act of love because God's favour or disfavour rests upon it.

We should remain in the churches we attend for as long as we can, engaging in the activities with a true sense of commitment, but the time may come when we are left with no choice but to leave a particular congregation. We may be asked to leave or else we may choose to do so because we feel we can stand it no longer. However, that should be the choice of last resort rather than the first.

Desperate Christians are often caught on the horns of a dilemma: if they leave a particular congregation, where do they go? After all, it cannot be right to live in isolation from other believers. We are members of the wider Body of Christ, when all is said and done, and so it is vital to maintain relationship as best we can because we are still identified as local Christians.

But we can only relate in *true* Kingdom life with those who are truly serving the King. For some a shift of perspective may be required. To see the local congregation not so much as our true 'Body' but more as our first line of mission. For those people it will be essential to seek out others similarly placed. Perhaps to form what were once referred to as 'cottage meetings': small groups of believers intent on following precisely the standards laid down in the New Testament: firmly resolved to grow mature as they share their lives, exposing themselves to the full glare of biblical truth, confessing their faults to one another and encouraging one another in the development of the fruit and gifts of the Holy Spirit.

Submitting to the others in such a group will enable us to grow into conquerors and that is essential. But we can still maintain a genuine relationship with local believers who at the moment may not be willing to go deeper, but who, when the truth dawns, may cry out for the fellowship and maturity we have been working towards. That will be the moment to embrace them and welcome them in.

All this is pretty confrontational. But is it what the Lord is asking of us? It is abundantly clear that basic changes have to be made if we are to be ready for the troubling times that are now upon us, let alone those that are rushing towards us. Are these proposals timely and are they viable?

Dare we even think about it?

(For further reading see "Hebraic Church" by Steve Maltz)

Chapter Eleven

Time for action!

Placing one foot on the river bank and the other in a dinghy is a risky position in which to place yourself! If you don't commit yourself completely either to standing securely on the bank or stepping out strongly across the gap and into the boat, you're sunk … literally!

Here is a challenge that is being faced by many believers at the present time. They are aware that just when authentic, vibrant faith needs to be encouraged and exercised and when true body-life needs to be built up and expressed, many organised churches are failing them … **dis**organised ones too!

We can thank the Lord that this is not universally true and there are church fellowships where remarkable strides in personal holiness and sound doctrine are being matched by powerful ministry. This, after all, is the clear purpose for His Church that Jesus inspired Paul to express in 1 Corinthians 12:27, *"Now you are the body of Christ, and each one of you is a part of it."*

When we think of the Lord Jesus, we think of His character *and* His ministry. When people met Him, they encountered both His holy character and His powerful good works, welded together as one. To encounter Jesus was to be overwhelmed by who He was *and* what He did for you. It was impossible to separate the two.

When Bartimaeus of Jericho encountered the Lord Jesus, he cried out, *"Jesus, Son of David, have mercy on me!"* (Mark 10:46-52). Bartimaeus acknowledged that Jesus was the Messiah, the Son of David, but also, on the basis of that, he expected to receive mercy: namely, healing of his blindness. And he did!

Our Lord's holy character was expressed supremely in love and the expression of that love was through His ministry. This is the principle by which the Father Himself operates. We see it in John 3:16, *"For God so **loved** ... that He **gave"**.* This astonishing statement reveals that God's love was expressed through a gift: namely, the gift of His dear Son. The God of love expressed that love by means of the gift.

When the divine Son was here He showed His holy character as He ministered to people. The evidence of the holiness of Jesus was the exercise of His ministry gifts and the way in which people received God's grace through them.

Bartimaeus was clearly aware of our Lord's messiahship (note his cry, *"Son of David"*) and on that basis he cried out to Him with urgency and confidence. He needed to receive the love of God. But how was it delivered? Our Lord did not respond to Bartimaeus by saying,

"Bartimaeus, you dear deprived man, I love you so much! Can you feel the warmth of my love flowing over you? Soak in it and let it warm you! Go in peace and allow the knowledge that I love you to transform your sad state by giving you grace to accept it!"

That is NOT what happened in Jericho that day! Jesus HEALED him! THAT'S what happened! It was his complete healing that was the evidence of our Lord's love for Bartimaeus.

It is striking that when Paul speaks of the *"Body of Christ"* he has two things in mind: the Fruit of the Spirit (expounded in Galatians 5:22 and 23) and the Gifts of the Spirit (expounded in 1 Corinthians 12 – 14). The truly functioning Church is a manifestation of holiness *and* power: the power motivated by holiness and the holiness issuing forth in mighty works of God.

Jesus nudged this remarkable fact into a further orbit of revelation when He said, *"Upon this rock I will build My Church and the gates of hell will not overcome it."* (Matthew 16:18)

This foundational "rock" is Peter's astonishing statement, inspired by the Holy Spirit, that Jesus is Messiah – our Great High Priest and King – the Son of the living God.

Our Lord goes on to describe the purpose of His Church: *"the gates of hell will not overcome it"*. In Greek and Hebrew the word "gates" carries the idea of "authorities".

The reason for this concerns ancient city gates which were the location of seats of authority where judges and kings could be consulted.

The words, *"will not overcome it"* also carry the meaning, *"will not be able to withstand it"*.

This is fighting talk! This is open warfare! Unpopular or not, this is our Lord's expectation of YOU and ME! The Church *Jesus* builds is engaging Satan's authorities by successfully attacking them and successfully defending itself against them.

Such, then, is the nature of the true Church that Jesus builds. Such a church will impact the society in which it is placed ... and does! Praise the Lord!

If you, dear Reader, are a member of such a local church, BE VERY GLAD! Many of your brothers and sisters do not have that privilege and are spiritually depressed as a result. They are trapped by religion and have a gnawing sense of deep frustration matched by personal guilt: they know full well what our Father expects of them, but it simply is not happening for them *and time is passing*!

When we face extreme challenges, extreme measures may be called for. It may be that even after years of trying to bring biblical correctives to bear in our church, there is unwillingness in the leadership to face the truth and the situation is now beyond remedy or redress. In such a sad circumstance is it not appropriate to call to mind the words of Peter and the apostles on two occasions when they were required by the religious authorities to compromise their position? Acts 4:19-20 and 5:29 describe parallel events. In the first the Jewish elders and teachers of the law commanded the apostles not to speak or teach at all in the name of Jesus. Peter and John replied, *"Judge for yourselves whether it is right in God's sight to obey you rather than God. For we cannot help speaking about what we have seen and heard."*

In the second, we find a follow-up in which the High Priest and Sanhedrin repeat their orders not to teach in Jesus' name. The reply of the apostles is straight to the point: *"We must obey God rather than men."*

What is the issue at stake? Plainly to obey the Word of God or to compromise. A stark choice but a clear one.

Whilst it is obviously true that the opposition in Acts was Jewish Orthodoxy, the issue is no different from that facing many of our Christian brethren in some churches today. Religion is the enemy of God's Word. Believers are being asked to believe doctrines of men rather than biblical doctrine and to live in the realm of religion rather than the life style of the Church Jesus builds.

When the pressure to compromise biblical truth reaches the point of no return, we are required to make painful choices in order to live for Jesus.

Given the urgency of the hour, truth has to be faced and it has to be responded to. But herein lies a problem. Who wants to leap from the frying pan into the fire? Or, to keep to our illustration of the dinghy, who wants to drop into the drink? Suppose we make a leap for safety without ensuring a secure landing place, what will become of us?

For many of us this is the nub of the problem and so we stay put and lose our fire. Fear and insecurity paralyse us.

At a time in my life when I had the privilege of preparing young people for marriage, I always used to say, "In order to cleave you have to leave!" By this I meant that if they were to make a success of their marriage they must put their spouse first and no longer their parents. The old single life was over and a new life beckoned that had to be set free in order to thrive.

Following Jesus will mean leaving past religious controls and restraints and throwing myself upon Him: living only by His Word in company with others so minded.

The worst possible state is to fall between the bank and the boat.
-     Leaving relationships behind but not finding new ones.
-     Leaving organised worship and teaching but not finding a living substitute.
-     Leaving organised, formal prayer but allowing personal devotions to be squeezed out.

-    Leaving church programmes behind but failing to engage with the society around.

Such might well be the fate of folks pulling away from local churches. BUT IT DOES NOT HAVE TO BE THAT WAY.

A little while ago I came across a remarkable book that addresses this situation head-on. It was written in 1996 but is bang up-to-date. It is a most encouraging little volume written by Stan Firth, a brother who took the step out of the boat, across the gap and into a place of deep security. As I read the opening chapter, I began to tremble! This man was speaking to ME! Let me quote,

"Over the years I have been coming across believers who are indisputably enthusiastic about Jesus Christ, and about serving Him in the world, but who no longer 'go to church'! They have given up the practice of regular, corporate worship and are not engaged in the usual, church activities. It is impossible, however, to categorise them as 'backsliders', for they continue in their personal devotion to Christ and seem to display the generally accepted characteristics of Christian discipleship – except in the whole area of church life ...

... for quite some time I asked myself what I should make of this unusual breed of Christians. Were they just a harmless minority lifestyle which could safely be left to co-exist alongside the other churches? On the other hand, did they represent a dangerous trend, against which other

Christians should be warned? Or could it be that they had something to say to the Church in general? ...

... Those I questioned from various parts of the world seemed to reply in similar vein, 'We consider the Church of Jesus Christ to be vitally important, both world-wide and locally, but we see it as "unstructured rather than structured". We believe our calling is to an UNSTRUCTURED CHURCH LIFESTYLE."

What rang bells with me is that the New Testament churches were like that. Is it too radical to ask if the Lord is calling us back to this?

Can we risk asking big questions as we face these Last Days with all their attendant challenges? Should we maintain the *status quo*? Or is there another way?

Think it through … and act!

Chapter Twelve

A need for discernment

I met a woman quite recently who scared me half to death! She did not appear particularly fierce on first acquaintance, but I became increasingly uneasy as we spoke. Here was a lady who was passionate about things related to the End Times and for that I commend her, but there was an obsessional quality about her remarks and attitude that troubled me immensely. She was very demanding and I could almost believe she was trying to manipulate me into preaching according to *her* agenda!

On the face of it she appears to be a good Christian with a stated regard for the Bible, but I fear that her fascination with Antichrist and his counter culture of demonic activity could be leading her away from the Throne of Grace. She has no discernible joy.

It made me think of Paul when he was evangelising Philippi. There was not a strong Jewish presence in that great Graeco-Roman city when Paul was there. In fact there were not sufficient Jewish men in town to form a synagogue. You needed ten Jewish men and there were clearly not enough because in Acts 16:13 Luke tells us that Paul, Silas and Timothy, together with Luke (the author) went outside the city gate to the river, where they expected to find "a place of prayer". With less than ten men in a town, Jewish residents had to content themselves with an open-air Sabbath prayer gathering.

The particular incident that was brought to mind was the encounter Paul had with a slave girl on the streets of Philippi. Luke describes the encounter in some detail. Acts 16:16-18 makes it clear that she was demonised. Clairvoyance was a manifestation of it. But what is intriguing is that *the spirits that spoke through her spoke the **truth**!*

"These men are servants of the Most High God, who are telling you the way to be saved."

There is nothing wrong with that statement, yet it was demonically inspired. This is uncomfortable stuff. We are inclined to believe that Satan is the father of lies and we are right to believe it. John 8:44 is unequivocal, *"He was a murderer from the beginning, not holding to the truth, for there is no truth in him. When he lies he speaks his native language, for he is a liar and the father of lies."*

Jesus said that, so we'd best believe it. Satan is a liar and he thrives on lies, but sometimes he departs from his normal activity and for his own ends tempts with truth – even biblical truth.

The slave girl was shouting her message day after day. The people of Philippi must have been quite astounded. Such a remarkable prophetic gift should surely be acknowledged by Paul and company as being evidence of a true gift from the Holy Spirit. Best make her a Minister of the town's embryonic church! Then again, perhaps not!

Luke says *"She kept this up for many days. Finally Paul became so troubled that he turned round and said to the spirit, 'In the name of Jesus Christ I command you to come out of her!' At that moment the spirit left her."*

Did you notice that Paul did not have instantaneous discernment? It took many days to develop. Once it did he acted decisively.

I am always impressed by believers that have instant discernment. They know instinctively when something is of the Lord and when it is not. Very impressive. I infrequently get that kind of discernment and wish it was more regular, but *gradual* discernment is something I have much more often. I meet a person who I think initially is a lovely believer and I am almost persuaded to "give myself to them"; but the longer I spend in their company the more uneasy I get. It may be what they say or something in their demeanour. Sometimes just a hint of something that gives a check: a doubt. I can feel guilty because of such doubts. Surely this is not becoming in a true believer. I should be so full of love and grace that I reject such negative thoughts about this person. But here they come again: "Be careful, Chris. Do not trust yourself to this person: there is something amiss here: What they are saying sounds good but it is *not* good: there is something behind it that could lead you astray: that voice you hear is not from heaven."

The discernment we recognise in Paul is elevated to its highest level in Jesus Himself. I'm always intrigued by that surprising comment by John (John 2:24-25), *"Now while He was in Jerusalem at the Passover Feast, many people saw the miraculous signs He was doing and believed in His name. But **Jesus would not entrust Himself to them**, for He knew all men. He did not need man's testimony about man, for He knew what was in a man."*

Jesus had the divine discernment to know true faith from spurious faith. Many people were impressed by His miraculous signs but the "faith" they exercised varied between genuine faith and superficial faith that was little more than excitement over signs and wonders.

To understand the truth about a person's spiritual state is not a natural ability. Only the Holy Spirit can give true discernment in assessing genuine faith. But He *can* give that discernment and He *does* give it.

In the skirmishes between Jesus and Satan in the Wilderness we have the classic example. A careful reading of Matthew 4:1-11 suggests that our Lord's discernment grew with each temptation. The first temptation casts doubt upon what the Father had just said to Jesus: *"This is my Son, whom I love; with Him I am well pleased"* (Matthew 3:17).

Turning stones to bread would confirm our Lord's Sonship. The tempter's ploy was to imply that God's Word by itself was insufficient and must be backed up by a clear miracle that the true Son of God would be able to perform. Such a demonstration of power would establish Jesus' Sonship. The tempter's venomous suggestion was that Father's Word was not sufficient.

Whenever we encounter deception, sooner rather than later the Word of God will be seen to be the main issue. As will the assurance of our standing before God.

There is another subtlety here. The tempter was insinuating the doubt, "If you cannot perform signs and wonders you are no Son of God!"

In the second temptation (Matthew 4:5-7) the tempter actually quotes Scripture in his attempt to nudge Jesus a step further away from His Father's Word! Is it possible? Clearly, yes. And here we see the danger of accepting uncritically those who can quote isolated Scriptures to justify their position. It sounds very convincing, but the Holy Spirit will give discernment if we compare Scripture with Scripture and open ourselves to the inner witness that comes from the Lord when we are hungering and thirsting for righteousness.

The third temptation takes us another step further. Whatever Jesus' appreciation of His experience in the Wilderness, He is now completely aware of who He is dealing with. "Get away from Me, Satan!" Worship is what the devil has been after all along! With the promise of power and status Satan does not even cloak his true motive. He thinks it will be enough to serve his purpose of diverting Jesus. You can understand the devil's reasoning because that strategy worked with so many others throughout biblical history who lay claim to be true servants of God and it was working equally well with so many who lived in Jesus' time. Inadvertently many were worshipping Satan. When the promise of power and status comes along, so many of us today also find it irresistible and our response is to bow to Satan.

The only course of action is that revealed by the Saviour: *"Worship (obey with total obedience) the Lord your God, and serve Him only!"*

Such is possible only when we are saturated in the written Word of God and living in the truth of it. It is our safeguard: the only attack and defence weapon we have against the wiles of the devil (see Ephesians 6:17). Our Lord needed nothing more, neither do we.

In these days when deception is a major challenge to believers, we must be diligent to be men and women of the Word and Spirit. Satan is out to divert us for his own ends. A favourite stratagem is to divert us into particular areas of biblical revelation to the exclusion of others. Israel is one example: End Times is another. There is a way that leads us to correct doctrine and a way that does not. I seem to encounter too many folks that have allowed themselves to become seriously out of balance doctrinally because they have been beguiled into particular Bible topics to the neglect of others.

At the present time there is a tendency in some to be so taken up with Antichrist and the world of the demonic that they are taking their eyes off the Lord of Glory. Satan is happy about that!

We can so easily point the finger at brothers and sisters who have fallen foul of and been diverted by (for instance) Emerging Church and the New Spirituality and quite overlook our own predilections.

By all means let us put Israel in her proper place according to the Bible. By all means let us prepare ourselves for the coming of the Lord Jesus at the Rapture. By all means let us look for the signs that are setting the scene for the emergence of Antichrist. But we are required to be men and women of the Truth, the *whole* Truth and *nothing* but the Truth.

We need to pray, "Lord, in Your mercy and grace give me clear-sightedness as to *Your* priorities so that I may walk wisely, living by your Word and Spirit and exercising true discernment in my dealings with others."

If I pray that way, there will be consequences! Best get ready for them!

Chapter Thirteen

A knowing child ... is that me?

Remember those days? The children in the back of the car. Five minutes into the journey. Having to fob them off with "Not yet, darlings ... but we'll be there *very* soon! Promise!"

Ah, yes: those were the days! Mind you, little seems to change in that regard. Our *grandchildren* say precisely the same thing ... and in exactly the same tone, the little darlings: "Aren't we there *yet*? I'm *bored*!"

As we progress through these End Days, something strangely similar rises in my heart. All around me the pillars that supported our society are crumbling with alarming speed and I wonder how long it can be before the Lord comes again. A question dominates my thinking increasingly and you may guess what it is: "Are we nearly there, Father?"

According to Mark 13:26-27 and 32-33, our Lord Jesus said concerning the day of his coming, *"At that time men will see the Son of Man coming in clouds with great power and glory. And he will send His angels and gather His elect from the four winds, from the ends of the earth to the ends of the heavens ...* **No-one knows about that day or hour,**

not even the angels in heaven, nor the Son, but only the Father. *Be on guard! Watch and pray! You do not know when that time will come."*

Our Father in Heaven holds the key, so it seems that our only recourse is Father Himself. If He chooses to keep silent on the matter for the time being, there is nothing more to be said. But Jesus gave clear directive as to the attitude we should adopt during the time that will precede His glorious return. *"Be on guard! Watch and pray!"*

There is a tendency amongst many believers to undermine their own faith by sitting loose on the amazing and obvious fact that our Father God is *Sovereign*. He, the great Creator, is omnipotent, omniscient and omnipresent. Father really does *know*! Such a glorious Father inspires confidence in His children! No wonder Abraham was told by divine revelation, *"Is **anything** too hard for the Lord?"* (Genesis 18:14). Faith answers, ***"NO!"***

When the children ask "Are we nearly there, Daddy?" they do so because they have faith that their dad knows where they are going and will get them there. They may moan a little (or a lot!) about the journey but they trust him for the destination.

That confident trust is born of relationship. They *know* their Dad.

When we know the Lord it breeds a level of trust that transcends *credal* faith. To know *about* the Lord is a poor substitute for knowing *Him.*

Our Lord introduced His High Priestly prayer with a glorious definition of eternal life: *"Now this is eternal life: that they might know You, the only true God, and Jesus Christ, whom You have sent."* (John 17:3)

It is this intimate relationship which underlies the faith we see in the Scriptures. So my question is, do I know the Father? If I do not, it is most tragic because Father's heart is bursting for that level of bonding. The apostle John was overwhelmed with that awareness. He wrote, *"How great is the love the Father has lavished on us, that we should be called children of God!"*

That's wonderful isn't it? But according to some early translations, it's not the complete statement! For instance, William Tyndale's great translation has, *"How great is the love the Father has lavished on us, that we should be called children of God AND THAT IS WHAT WE **ARE**!*

When a child is deprived of his father through separation, he will often be heard to observe in later life, "I never *knew* my father". I did not know my own Dad until I was two years old. I was born during World War II when my Dad was away from home. He was a Sergeant Major in the Royal Artillery and when I was an infant he was fighting in France, Belgium and Germany. During those tough years all he saw of me was photos that Mum sent over. He cherished her letters that described in great detail the antics of his little son! I was fortunate to have an Uncle who lived with us. He worked for a munitions factory in Yeovil and so was excused Army service. I doted on Uncle Claude.

When my Dad was demobbed and came home, I didn't know who he was. At first sight, when he attempted to pick me up, I screamed the house down. Who was this stranger? I wanted my Uncle Claude.

It took a while for me to bond with my Daddy. But once established, we were utterly devoted to each other. No man could love me more than Dad and he became the centre of my world. All other dads were compared with my Dad, and they didn't match up too well! That, at any rate, was my perception as a growing child.

As I have been thinking about my need to know my Heavenly Father, that childhood experience has moved me. Dad wasn't around but my Uncle was. I loved my uncle and he was a dear, but he wasn't Dad. In a sense, for all Uncle Claude's affection for me, it steered me in a wrong direction. It was then hard to make the transition when Dad came home.

Have we become so used to substitutes for Father God that we find it hard to relate to *Him*?

Many are the books that have been written, many the messages preached about the Father-heart of God and our need to know Him and love Him. I wonder how effective they are in your experience? If I were to ask you, is your relationship with Father based upon knowledge *about* Him or knowledge *of* Him, I wonder how you would respond.

It is knowledge of God as Father that enabled Paul to stand strong when he faced his fearsome challenges and urged others to do the same.

Paul's letters to the Thessalonians were written in the white heat of persecution. Christians were persevering against tremendous odds. Paul thought so highly of the forbearance of the Thessalonians that he wrote, *"... among God's churches we boast about your perseverance and faith in all the persecutions and trials you are enduring"* (2 Thessalonians 1:4). Theirs was a powerful testimony.

"So then, brothers, stand firm and hold to the teachings we passed on to you, whether by word of mouth or by letter." (2 Thessalonians 2:15)

We're all good at *talking* tough *before* opposition explodes but Paul was addressing a situation in Thessalonica where the explosion had already happened and believers were facing the fall-out: outright persecution in various kinds of trials. What a trial of faith. What a temptation to shelter from persecution by hiding away behind the shield of apostasy.

Paul was anxious in case his friends should slither away from the clear teachings they had received from him. His anxiety was not based upon nothing. The temptation to compromise for the sake of peace was overwhelming and so Paul made it his business to "lay it on the line" and move every muscle to keep his friends centred in Father and in Jesus.

As then, so now: it is time to stand strong. We might fondly suppose that persecution is a distant prospect and while we acknowledge its presence in far off lands and cultures, we cannot recognise it in our own. It is no longer the case. Persecution both subtle and not so subtle is confronting us continually if we open our eyes to see it for what it is. We are surrounded by tremendous threats to solid, biblical faith: even from certain strands of Evangelical Christianity. The tragedy is that so many of us in choosing not to recognise it are choosing the way of compromise with society and with organised Church life.

Make no mistake, the fiercest opposition to biblical faith may well come from organised religion rather than the State. And by "religion" I do not necessarily mean Islam, Hinduism and the like. The clear and present danger is also what Paul refers to as "apostasy" (2 Thessalonians 2:3). This literally means "falling away", although some translations choose "rebellion".

Paul uses *apostasia* to refer to a falling away from Father God around the same time that the "man of lawlessness" emerges to dominate the world stage. So when we see a wholesale turning from God's Word and the dishonouring of King Jesus, the rise of Antichrist cannot be far away.

"Falling away" implies a falling down from a higher state. Clearly it points to society at large and also to the visible Church. In our society we have a glorious history of which the Bible formed the bedrock. Not any more. God is progressively written out of our nation's life at every level. Britain has fallen away from God. Britain is not only '*Post*-Christian' it is now decidedly '*Anti*-Christian'.

But what of Christian faith itself? In the life of many churches, significant numbers of God's great truths are being discarded as incompatible with modern thought. Inconvenient truths are being set aside for the sake of peaceful coexistence with 21st Century opinion. Many are frantic not to be seen as out of step with current trends. Numbers of British churches (and individual Christians) have fallen away from God by varying degrees. So apostasy and persecution are no longer distant prospects: they are clear and present dangers.

The positive message of Paul is *"stand firm and hold to the teachings we passed on to you, whether by word of mouth or by letter."* There was a consistent message that came through Paul when physically present and also when absent. His preaching and letter writing were one. He communicated the unadulterated Word of God in the power of the Holy Spirit.

Most folks in our churches hate uncomfortable truth. Smooth things are more in their line. But however unpopular and unpalatable our message, we really have no choice except to proclaim it if we are to be faithful to the call of the Lord.

A while ago I wrote a book entitled "Speak Lord … but who's listening?" I felt a heavy burden from the Lord to speak out what I genuinely believed (and still believe) to be a burden on His heart: He wants His children back and He wants His Church back. If you have a sense that it is something you need to read, please see our advert at the end of this book.

A trap that threatens the unwary Evangelical is to confuse being a man of the Word with knowing Father. The two should be one, but so often are not. I have met many powerful Christians that are "big Bible men and women". You only have to ask them a question regarding the Bible, the nature of God and the life of faith and they will amaze you with their erudition. My question is, "Do they know the Father?" But there is a further question, "My dear reader, do *you* know the Father?"

Then again there is the ultimate question. "Do *I*, Chris Hill, know the Father?" According to the Lord Jesus, that's the confirming evidence of my eternal life … or not.

Know God? Know God as 'Father'? Dare we settle for less? It's time to seek Him!

May the Father, Son and Spirit bless you as you do it.

BOOKS AND CDs REFERRED TO IN THE TEXT

The One New Man Bible (book)
translated by William J Morford   £40.00

Custom and Command (book)
by Stan Firth   £5.00

Preaching and Preachers (book)
by Martyn Lloyd-Jones   £8.99

Hebraic Church (book)
by Steve Maltz   £10.00

Built for Battle (book)
by Chris Hill   £10.00

Speak, Lord ... but who's listening? (book)
by Chris Hill   £10.00

Saul of Tarsus (booklet)
by Chris Hill   £2.00

Going for Gold (booklet)
by Chris Hill   £2.00

The Word, the Spirit and the Witnesses (set of 2 CDs)
by Chris Hill   £8.00

These items may be ordered (Postage extra) from
C L Ministries

Why not join Chris and Lindy Hill on one of their renowned Bible tours of

Israel?

Experience gained through over thirty years of leading Israel tours makes Chris one of today's foremost tour leaders. He and Lindy have led ninety six tours during those years and several thousand people have joined them. Many of these folk return for a second tour! Some, indeed, have been with the Hills on as many as *five* occasions!

Scheduled flights, excellent hotels and coaches, together with a highly experienced Jewish Guide, guarantee a secure and rich experience. Chris's Bible teaching in each location visited brings the Word of God to life and the whole memorable experience enriches the faith of those who come.

Publications and Tour brochures available from

C L Publications

28 Thorney Road, Capel St Mary, Suffolk IP9 2LH
Tel: 01473 311128 Email: clministries@btinternet.com
www.clministries.org.uk